CROSSROADS 2

CROSSROADS 2

TEACHER'S BOOK

Barbara J. Sample

with

Earl W. Stevick

and

Spring Institute for International Studies

Oxford University Press

Oxford University Press
200 Madison Avenue
New York, NY 10016 USA

Walton Street
Oxford OX2 6DP England

OXFORD is a trademark of Oxford University Press.

ISBN 0-19-434382-0

Editorial Manager: Susan Lanzano
Editors: Jane Sturtevant, Patricia Nardiello
Associate Editor: Allen Appel
Designer: Sharon Hudak
Art Buyer/Picture Researcher: Karen Polyak
Production Controller: Abram Hall

Cover illustration by Dennis Ziemienski

Illustrations by Bob Marstall

Printing (last digit): 10 9 8 7 6 5 4 3 2 1

Printed in the United States.

Contents

Introduction

Where to find it in the Introduction

Who is Crossroads for?

CROSSROADS is for adults and young adults who are in adult education and continuing education programs. These adults have diverse linguistic and cultural backgrounds, educational levels, learning styles, occupational histories, and hopes for the future. They need to learn English so that they can function fully in our society in all their roles: as workers, parents, consumers, and members of their communities.

CROSSROADS is for real beginners, including those with very limited literacy in English, or literate in a language that uses a non-Roman alphabet. CROSSROADS begins lower and progresses more slowly than most beginning series.

Which level of Crossroads is right for my students?

Place students in CROSSROADS 1 if they function minimally or not at all in English. Students may be able to express a limited number of immediate survival needs using simple learned phrases, but it is very difficult to communicate with them, even when relying heavily on gestures.

Place students in CROSSROADS 2 if they are able to function in a very limited way in English to meet their immediate needs. At this level, students are employable only in routine, entry-level jobs in which all tasks can be demonstrated.

Place students in CROSSROADS 3 if they have moved beyond a limited range of learned phrases, and are beginning to function with some independence and creativity. They speak with hesitation, need assistance, and have difficulty communicating with someone who is not used to dealing with people of limited English proficiency.

Place students in CROSSROADS 4 if they can communicate, although with difficulty, on familiar topics with native speakers who are not accustomed to dealing with people of limited English proficiency.

CROSSROADS is compatible with the Comprehensive Adult Student Assessment System (CASAS) and the Student Performance Levels (SPL's) recommended by the Mainstream English Language Training (MELT) Project of the U.S. Department of Health and Human

Services. SPL's are correlated with scores on the Basic English Skills Test (BEST).

	MELT SPL's	BEST Scores	CASAS Achievement Scores
CROSSROADS 1	I and II	9–28	165–190
CROSSROADS 2	III	29–41	191–196
CROSSROADS 3	IV and V	42–57	197–210
CROSSROADS 4	VI and VII	58–65+	211–224

Placement can also be made according to students' control of grammar. CROSSROADS 1 covers the present tense of be, the present continuous tense, and the simple present tense. CROSSROADS 2 covers the past tense of *be* and regular verbs, and the future with *be + going to.* CROSSROADS 3 covers the past tense with irregular verbs, the future tense with *will,* and the past progressive tense. CROSSROADS 4 covers the present perfect and present perfect continuous tenses.

What does Crossroads teach?

CROSSROADS integrates its grammar syllabus with a competency-based approach. Competencies are discrete, measurable skills students need in order to function in this society. They can be grouped into topics such as health, employment, transportation, social language, and community services. Competencies may require listening comprehension *(Follow instructions in a medical exam)*, speaking *(Report an emergency)*, reading *(Read street signs)*, or writing *(Write your address)*. Competencies increase in complexity with each level of CROSSROADS. A Level 1 competency in the unit called Housing is *Name rooms in a house.* A Level 4 competency in the same topic is *Ask and answer questions about a lease.*

Students immediately begin to develop basic communicative competency in specific areas that are essential to their functioning in this society. At the same time, they gain control of how English works, so that they can use what they've learned in new and unexpected situations.

Vocabulary, listening, and reading and writing are built into each unit of CROSSROADS. Document literacy (for coping with the blizzard of forms adults are faced with) gets special attention. Pronunciation is an integral part of speaking and listening work, and is treated in detail in the Teacher's Book.

What is in Student Book 2?

The Student Book has ten consistently-organized units, each based on a topic such as Housing, Health, or Transportation. The Table of Contents provides an overview of the topics, competencies, and grammar in each unit.

Each 12-page unit consists of the following sections, described below:

Getting Started (1 page)
Conversations (3 pages)
Paperwork (1 page)
Reading and Writing (2 pages)
Listening Plus (1 page)
Interactions (2 pages)
Progress Checks (1 1/2 pages)
Memo to the Teacher (1/2 page)

GETTING STARTED

The first page of each unit introduces the unit topic and establishes a context for new material. Pictures show characters involved in a situation, such as renting an apartment, enrolling in adult school, or having an accident at work. Students guess what the characters might be saying, listen to the conversation on cassette, and then tell the teacher what they've heard.

CONVERSATIONS

The situation pictured on the Getting Started page unfolds on the Conversations pages. In exercises called *Practice,* students guess what is being said in a conversation, listen to the conversation on cassette, say what they can recall of it, listen again while they read it, and finally practice saying it. These model conversations present grammatical structures and competencies.

New grammatical structures are highlighted in exercises called *Focus on Grammar,* which concentrate students' attention on some feature of how English works. Language samples are expanded into substitution tables, simple drills, and pair practice. Students gain insight into grammatical forms without using grammar terms.

What can you say? exercises use pictures to expand vocabulary introduced in *Practice.* Students learn what the new words mean and work on sight-reading and writing them before using them in communicative exercises.

Once the new competencies, grammar, and vocabulary are in place, students practice them in structured conversation exercises, incorporating personal information wherever appropriate. Many of these exercises are called *Talk about....* Many Level 2 students cannot understand detailed instructions in English, so students see the exercise demonstrated by you and by volunteers, then try the exercise first as choral repetition, and finally practice it in several different pairs or groups.

Some exercises carry a letter in the margin. The letter indicates that the exercise provides the first varied practice of a specific competency. The same letters appear in the Progress Checks pages at the end of the unit, where the competencies are identified by name and in the Competency Checklists on pages 112–131 of the Teacher's Book. If a student has missed class or needs additional practice with a given competency, refer her to the exercise with the corresponding letter.

LISTENING PLUS

Listening comprehension skills are developed through a variety of listening tasks.

Certain exercises involve listening to conversations at a level that students are not expected to comprehend fully. The spoken material in these exercises is for listening only. You should not try to teach it, and the students should neither read it nor feel they must learn it.

PAPERWORK

Students learn to read and fill in simple forms like those they encounter in their daily lives. They also interview each other, practicing questions that are common in interviews for jobs, schools, and social services.

READING AND WRITING

The first activity on each Reading and Writing page is a pre-reading activity. This is followed by the reading itself and a comprehension check exercise.

In Student Book 2, readings are longer than in Student Book 1 and appear in standard paragraph form. However, Level 2 students may still be struggling with reading. For this reason, all readings are on cassette and use no grammar and very little vocabulary that students have not already practiced orally. (By Book 4, students are expected to learn new vocabulary through context and to read passages and write compositions several paragraphs long.)

The reading serves as a model for the writing activities that follow. Students first do pre-writing activities, which include talking to a partner about what they will write. The writing tasks are practical and, whenever appropriate, students write about themselves. After writing, students read their work aloud in a group and get feedback from their peers.

INTERACTIONS

The Interactions pages provide information gap exercises, which create a need for communication. Each student in a pair has information the other needs to complete a task. The object of the exercise is for each student to communicate his information to his partner, without showing her his page.

PROGRESS CHECKS

At the end of each unit are Progress Checks, which allow you and the students to find out how well they have mastered the competencies presented in the unit. Even if your program is not competency-based, these exercises are a useful way for students to demonstrate that they have acquired the language taught in the unit.

Each exercise tests a specific competency or competencies, identified here by letter and by name. You can evaluate students yourself, have peers evaluate each other, or have students evaluate themselves. These options are discussed more fully in the section on the roles of the teacher.

The two-part exercises called *What are the people saying?/Do it yourself* are unique to CROSSROADS. In *What are the people saying?*, students work in pairs or alone to generate a conversation based on what they have practiced in the unit. They are prompted by pictures, and some of the words and sentences are supplied. This part of the exercise provides a review of what students have practiced, and also lets them demonstrate how well they control the grammatical structures involved. *What are the people saying?* can be done orally or in writing. There is an answer key *(Basic Conversations)* for *What are the people saying?* in the back of the Student Book.

The second part of the exercise, *Do it yourself,* is where competency is demonstrated. The exercise is designed for classroom use. Therefore, since many competencies are required not in classrooms, but in stores, in the workplace, or elsewhere in the community, *Do it yourself* sometimes involves a degree of role playing and imagination. For example, to demonstrate the competency *Follow simple instructions for medical treatment,* students take the roles of doctor and patient. The "patient" mimes what the doctor says to do. When a competency requires reading *(Identify total due on monthly bills, Read sizes and prices on tags), Do it yourself* provides the material to be read.

MEMO TO THE TEACHER

This is a culminating activity to help bridge the gap between the relatively controlled and protected language environment of the classroom and the unpredictability of the outside world. The Memo suggestion on the last page of each Student Book unit can be carried out in the classroom. Options suggested in the Teacher's Book sometimes require students to actually leave the school and use English to complete a task in the community.

The Memo is not an evaluation tool like other exercises on the Progress Checks pages. It provides an opportunity for the student to bring his new language skills to bear on a fairly complex and extended task. Success is in the completion of the task, rather than in the accurate production of language.

What else does the Student Book offer?

STEP-BY-STEP TEACHING PROCEDURES

A section of Step-by-Step Teaching Procedures precedes Unit 1. The Procedures cover the majority of exercise types—all those that recur from unit to unit. These procedures use pictures, listening, choral repetition, and controlled practice to help you support the efforts of low-level students who may not be able to sight-read the conversations in the book; they end with personalization and more open-ended work in pairs and groups.

GRAMMAR SUMMARIES

Grammar Summaries in the back of the Student Book bring together, in the form of charts and complete paradigms, the discrete grammar points presented in the units. The Grammar Summaries are a convenient reference for you and may be useful to students whose learning styles are compatible with this kind of information.

TAPESCRIPT

Scripts for Listening Plus Exercises 1, 2, and 4, which are recorded on cassette, are printed in the back of the Student Book, so that you can preview exercises or read the scripts aloud if you do not use the cassette. Note that many other exercises are also on cassette, as indicated by the cassette symbols in the Student Book. Since the scripts for these exercises are part of the unit, they are not reprinted in the Tapescript.

BASIC CONVERSATIONS

This is an answer key for Progress Checks exercises called *What are the people saying?* Students may know other ways to demonstrate the competency, but the Basic Conversations give the language that was practiced in the unit.

What does the Teacher's Book offer?

UNIT NOTES

For each unit of the Student Book, the Teacher's Book provides:

- Reproducible versions of the first-page illustrations
- Warm-up activities
- Step-by-step instructions for every exercise, more detailed than those in the front of the Student Book
- Suggestions for varying or extending exercises
- Cross-cultural and linguistic notes and suggestions about classroom management
- Pronunciation exercises

- Cross-references to exercises in the CROSSROADS *Multilevel Activity and Resource Package*
- Cross-references to vocabulary pages in *The New Oxford Picture Dictionary.*

COMPETENCY CHECKLISTS

In the back of the Teacher's Book you will find reproducible Competency Checklists in two formats: for individual students and for the whole group. These will simplify your record keeping and help students appreciate how much they have learned.

Group Competency Checklists provide spaces for ten students to a page. There is room to record a date, a grade, or both for each student under each competency.

Individual Competency Checklists provide space for a more detailed record for a single student. Columns are not headed, so that you can fill in headings that best fit your needs. Here are some possibilities. The first two examples are for evaluation by the teacher, with grades given. The third is an example for peer testing, with two *OKs* out of three being a passing grade. (See page xv for more about peer testing.)

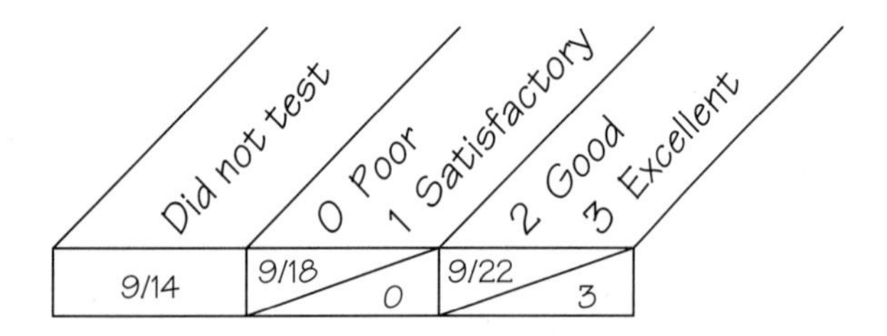

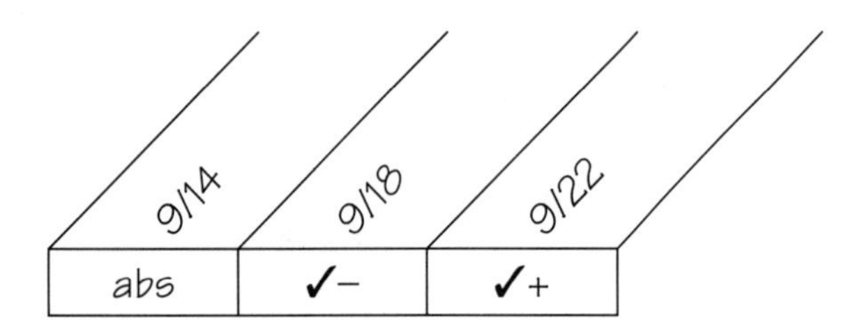

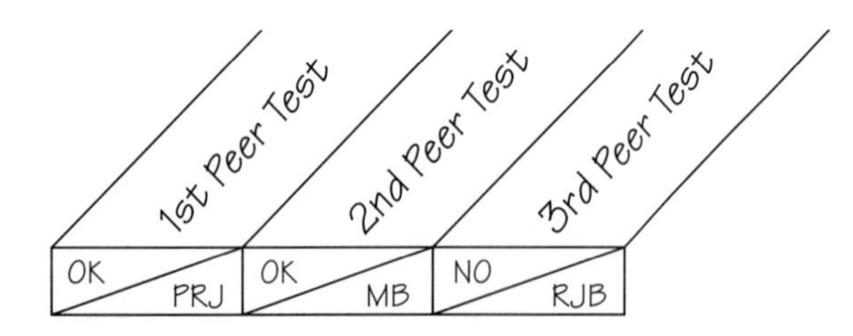

How can I use Crossroads with multilevel classes, open enrollment, and fluctuating attendance?

Although students may be placed in classes according to their levels, the reality is that most ESL classes are multilevel, whether because they are open-entry, or because students progress at different rates, or because students are not equally proficient in listening, speaking, reading, and writing. Here are some techniques for using CROSSROADS with multilevel classes:

- In activities that call for pair work, pair students who work faster with those who work slower.
- Use the worksheets or cards in the *Multilevel Activity and Resource Package,* or the cassettes, or your own prepared materials for students who finish activities before others. Set up a system so that students who finish early can get extra work easily and independently.
- Make a small group of students who need special attention. Work directly with the group while other students are occupied with material from the *Multilevel Activity and Resource Package* or with materials you have prepared yourself.
- Give additional responsibilities to students who are progressing faster. For example, have them put their answers on the board while others are still working at their seats.
- Set up peer tutoring for reading, writing, and vocabulary practice. Again, the *Multilevel Activity and Resource Package* provides ideal materials. Have tutors work with material they have already completed. Coach tutors so that they really help, rather than just giving the answers.

TEACHING VOCABULARY TO LOW-LEVEL STUDENTS

In general, all you will need to do with new vocabulary is point to a picture in the Student Book. However, students may sometimes need more help, and students using CROSSROADS 2 may have little vocabulary in English that you can use to explain new words. If your students have the same first language, and you know it, using it occasionally can save time and frustration, while at the same time validating the students' culture. If translation is not an option, these strategies may be useful:

- Let other students translate or explain.
- Point to the actual thing, if it's in sight.
- Show pictures you have brought in.
- Draw simple pictures on the board.
- Act it out. If a student doesn't understand *Help!* (page 50), ham it up as you say *Help! There's an accident!, Help! There's a fire!*, or *Help! There's a robbery!*
- Give examples. If a student doesn't understand *community services,* tell her (or elicit from other students) the *Department of Motor Vehicles, the fire department, schools,* etc.
- Paraphrase or use a synonym. If a student doesn't understand *learner's permit* (page 26), point to the picture and say *It's a permission form. It says you can practice driving.*

  In some cases, it is more productive to deal with whole phrases than with isolated words. *Nice* is hard to get across, but *Nice to meet you* can be acted out very easily.

HELPING STUDENTS REVIEW OR MAKE UP MISSED WORK

When students are absent, or enter the class after the term has begun, or are unable to demonstrate a given competency in Progress Checks, you may wish to help them make up what they have missed, so that they do not fall behind the rest of the class. The most obvious way to do this is to sit down with the student after class and tutor her. In practice, however, few teachers can do this. Here are some techniques for using CROSSROADS for make-up work:

- Keep good records. Your Competency Checklist (photocopied from the back of the Teacher's Book) will tell you the date that a student demonstrated, or failed to demonstrate, each competency.
- If a student has not failed to demonstrate a competency, but has merely missed work, first see if she can demonstrate the competency without make-up work. Students often achieve some competency on their own.
- Consider reviewing the material for the whole class. Students need all the review they can get, even if most of them have already demonstrated competency. One way to do this without taking too much class time is to use missed work as a warm-up at the beginning of class.
- Use techniques such as peer tutoring or group work, recommended above for multilevel classes. A competency letter next to an exercise identifies the exercise as the best practice for the competency, and the best material for tutors.

How can I help my students with pronunciation?

Students expect and appreciate pronunciation work, although, at beginning levels, the greatest gains they make from it may be in *hearing* the sounds of English. The Teacher's Book suggests pronunciation work at appropriate points in each unit. Three different exercise types are recommended:

IMITATION AND CORRECTION

Beginning with a set of words on the board, students pronounce them and get direct feedback on the accuracy of their pronunciation.

The Teacher's Book recommends sets of words for practice and gives information about how to pronounce certain sounds in the words.

Step-by-Step

1. Write the recommended set of words on the board.
2. Point to one of the words and pronounce it, having students repeat after you as a whole group, in smaller groups, or individually.
3. Let students know how close their pronunciation comes to clear, easily understood English.
4. On the board, point to the part of the word that does not sound right. Form the sounds in an exaggerated way, or use your hands to mimic teeth and tongue to demonstrate how the sound should be produced.

MINIMAL PAIRS

Minimal pairs are words or phrases that differ in only one sound *(hear/ear, light/right)*. The Teacher's Book recommends a pair of words that students already know, or one that they know and another common word whose meaning can be easily demonstrated. For each minimal pair, there is a pair of responses, usually short, different-sounding sentences, each containing one word of the minimal pair. If the cues are *see* and *she,* then the responses can be *See you tomorrow* and *She's my friend* (page 6).

The Teacher's Book provides information about pronunciation of the sounds (what the tongue, teeth, and lips do; whether the voice is used, or just the breath), and which students (from which language backgrounds) might have trouble with them.

Step-by-Step

1. Write the minimal pair, one above the other, on one side of the board. Next to each word write the corresponding response. Have students practice saying the two responses several times.
2. Pronounce the two words clearly several times, in random order, pointing to each word as you say it.
3. Pronounce one of the words without pointing at it, and have students say the response corresponding to the word they think they heard. Then you point to the word you said. Do this with both words, in random order, until most of the students are giving the right response.
4. Have a volunteer come to the board, point to a word, and say it. You, meanwhile, have closed your eyes or turned your back. Give the response for the word you think you hear.
5. Let students give cues for other students as you did in Step 3.

THE HUMAN COMPUTER™

The Human Computer™ was originated by the late Dr. Charles A. Curran, the founder of Counseling-Learning/Community Language Learning*. It is one of many techniques (with multiple ways of being implemented depending upon the teaching context) associated with C-L/CLL. Each of these techniques was developed to encourage and empower students to be true to their unique learning needs and to take responsibility for their own learning process. In CROSSROADS, we recommend it as a pronunciation technique.

The premise of The Human Computer™ is that the teacher functions like a human computer—simultaneously sensitive to the students' needs (human), and non-judgmentally at the service of the students (like a computer). One group of six to eight students participates directly as the practice group, the "computer operators." The balance of the class is the overhear group.

In your explanation of The Human Computer ™ to the class before you begin, it is helpful to remind yourself that you are following the student's lead. Their choices determine what and how many times you pronounce something. You might use the students' first language, or explain the technique to a group of more advanced students, and then demonstrate it with them.

The activity begins with an announced time limit (usually five to ten minutes) and with a few sentences on the board to practice. It is helpful to the teacher, and fellow students as well, to number each sentence so students can refer to the number before they give their choice. Students in the practice group can choose anything on the board to work on—a sound, a word, a phrase, or a whole sentence—it's up to each individual. When a student knows what she wants to practice, she raises her hand and you stand behind her. The student pronounces whatever she wants to practice and you repeat in a clear, non-correcting, respectful way. The student listens to your pronunciation and compares it with her own. The student can continue, pronouncing either the same thing, or something else, or she can stop. When she stops, another student can take a turn.

Since students are used to repeating *after* the teacher, they may not know how to stop at first. If you enforce the time limit, even though some students in the practice group have not had a turn, students will quickly realize and even remind each other that it is up to them to stop.

While the practice group is operating The Human Computer™, students in the overhear group often recognize their own mistakes as they compare their classmates' pronunciation with The Human Computer's™. When it's their turn to be in the practice group, their pronunciation is likely to have improved. As time goes on, students become more aware of their own areas of difficul-

---

* For further information on The Human Computer™, see Jennybelle P. Rardin, et al., *Education in a New Dimension: The Counseling-Learning® Approach to Community Language Learning,* 1988, Counseling-Learning Publications, P. O. Box 285, East Dubuque, IL 61025.

ty, and become more selective about what pieces of language from the board they want to work on when they are in the practice group.

Step-by-Step

1. Have students look at the sentences on the board or overhead projector (OHP).
2. Choose a group of six to eight students for the practice group.
3. Tell students how much time they'll have for the activity.
4. Have students take turns pronouncing some part of the text on the board and listening to your repetition. The student decides whether to continue or stop.
5. When the time is up, thank the practice group, and repeat the activity with another group if you wish.

How can I vary the Basic Teaching Procedures?

In general, students welcome any opportunity to take over some of your tasks: to write on the board, demonstrate conversations, explain vocabulary, correct errors, etc. Teacher's Book unit notes suggest other ways to vary and extend specific exercises. In addition, here is a menu of options to choose from for some of the exercises (in alphabetical order) that recur throughout the Student Book:

Fill in the form.

- With a volunteer's information filled in on the board, have students ask each other questions about the volunteer, based on the form.
- After pairs have checked each other's forms, ask students questions about their partners.
- Have students question each other in the same way.
- Erase everything from the form on the board, point to the blanks, and give information for individual students. Make deliberate errors of fact and let students correct you.

Guess.

- Give students as long as 30 seconds to look at the picture before anyone says anything. This gives less talkative students time to rehearse mentally.
- Ask what the characters want and what they feel.
- Instead of responding orally to students' guesses, write them on the board.

Interview three classmates.

- Write the interview questions on the board and use The Human Computer™ to work on pronunciation before students interview each other.
- When you are interviewed, answer naturally. *(Where was I born? Was that your question? Oh, well, I was born in _____. That's near _____.)* Let the class help the interviewer decide which information answered the question.

Practice.

- Ask simple questions to check comprehension.
- Sometimes use individual repetition instead of choral repetition.
- When students are able to say the conversation easily, have volunteers act it out with emotions that are appropriate to the content: sadness, excitement, etc.

Read about _____.

- Let students use The Human Computer™ with the sentences in the story.
- Write a sentence from the reading on the board, but change one word. Have volunteers correct the sentence.
- Select words from the reading and let students practice spelling them. Have one volunteer write on the board as another spells.
- Write part of a sentence from the reading on the board (anything from one word to the sentence minus one word). Have volunteers complete the sentence, with or without looking at the book.
- Write five words on the board: four from the reading and one not from the reading. Point to each word and have students say whether it is in the reading or not. If it is, a volunteer reads aloud the sentence where it is found.

Review... Write... Number.

- Let students hear the conversations only once, but work in pairs to write the answers. As the tape plays, circulate and quickly check off correct answers. Finish checking papers before playing the tape again. (This works only in small classes.)
- Conversely, let students hear each conversation as many times as they wish.

- In a week, let students hear these conversations again and answer simple questions about them in pairs or groups *(Where are they? What is happening? What are they talking about?)*.

Talk about _____.

- See if students can find where to get needed information without your guidance.
- Take one of the roles in a conversation and make a "mistake" from time to time, letting students correct you.
- Take one part in a conversation and add authentic gestures, hesitations, and comments, without changing the basic content.
- In conversations with cues to be substituted, let students suggest additional cues.

Talk about your _____/yourself.

- When pairs demonstrate for the class, restate their information after each pair has spoken. Sound very interested in what they have said. Make occasional "mistakes" of fact for students to correct.
- Have other students restate what the volunteers have said.
- After practicing the exercise "straight," have student do it again with the most outrageous fictitious information they can invent.

What about you?

- Before students write, get them to respond orally. Say to a student, for example, *This woman's name is Donna Jones, and she's from Austin, Texas. What about you?*
- Do as above, but extend the practice. *And what about* (the preceding student)? *And what about* (the student before that one)?, etc.

What can you hear?

- After students hear the tape, ask the same questions as in *Guess.*
- Have students act out the conversation after hearing the tape once or twice, using anything they can say, whether from the tape or not.
- Write students' recollections on the board; then, in *Practice,* compare their suggestions with the conversation in the book.

What can you say?

- Give students only a few seconds to look at the pictures before closing their books and guessing as many words as they can.
- Invite questions about pronunciation. Use Imitation and Correction.
- Have students cooperate to recall the words without looking at the pictures.

What's next?

- Instead of pointing, have students respond orally.
- After listening, have students approximate the conversations as role plays, without referring to the tapescript.
- Do as above, and have students extend the conversations as much as they can.

Write about yourself.

- Students can respond to your story after each sentence, or after you have told the whole story.
- When students restate your story, write each piece of information on the board as they say it; then let a volunteer write your story on the board with the others collaborating, instead of writing it yourself.

What are the teaching principles underlying Crossroads?

ELICIT BEFORE YOU TEACH

Adults bring a wealth of knowledge and life experiences to learning. CROSSROADS acknowledges this by letting you elicit what students know before you teach them. This accomplishes three things: it gets students engaged in the activity, it gives you a chance to assess what they know, and it gives students "credit" for knowing something.

Some of the recurring exercises in CROSSROADS exemplify this principle: *Guess. What are they saying?* has students guess the content of a conversation, based on what they see in a picture and what they already know about the world. *What can you hear?* has students reconstruct a conversation they've just heard, and *What can you say?* has them name what they see in pictures before learning the items they don't know.

HELP STUDENTS REALIZE THAT IT'S GOOD TO TAKE RISKS

Speaking a new language, using unfamiliar gestures, and interacting with new people—these are some of the realities in the lives of beginning students. Each is an area where it's all too easy to be misunderstood, and where you, as a teacher, can make a tremendous difference. If you can make your students feel that it's all right to risk mistakes, then you will have removed a serious obstacle to their learning. Here are some ways you can encourage students to take risks:

- Dignify students' responses. When you elicit before you teach, students will be willing to offer answers if you accept their responses with appreciation, regardless of the correctness of the response. Simply restate the response in clear, grammatical English, or say the correct answer, focusing on the whole class and not on the individual who answered.
- Establish a supportive climate in the class by using group-forming activities, encouraging collaboration, and ensuring that students work with many different classmates. These suggestions are further explained in the section on the roles of the teacher.
- Have students work in small groups and pairs. Group and pair work diminishes students' sense of risk by giving them a chance to try things out in a less public way. In addition, these activities offer greater opportunities for real practice. In pair exercises, for example, half the students can be talking at the same time, whereas in whole-class work, only one student at a time can talk.

ENGAGE STUDENTS IN COMMUNICATIVE ACTIVITIES

CROSSROADS exercises follow a standard progression: new language is presented, students practice it in a controlled way, then they apply it to themselves. This allows students to engage in real communication and motivates them to master the new language. Some of the recurring exercises in CROSSROADS that exemplify this principle are *Talk about yourself, Interview three classmates, Write about yourself, Fill in the form,* and *What about you?*

RESPECT STUDENTS' RIGHT TO PRIVACY

Some students may wish to keep certain things about themselves private (their addresses, for example). Let students know that they may use either real or fictitious information in exercises that call for sensitive information.

Some students may not have real information to contribute. An unemployed student may have to use fictitious information in an exercise about occupations in order to get the benefit of the practice. Students may also use imaginary information just to be playful. By using imaginary information, they can take on different identities and may feel freer to take risks.

ACCOMMODATE DIFFERENT LEARNING STYLES

Learners acquire knowledge in different ways. Some learners need to see things, while others need to hear things; some need to get their information from an authority, while others will listen only to peers; some need to work cooperatively, while others need to work alone.

CROSSROADS accommodates all these learning styles. New material is introduced both with pictures and through listening. Activities include physical response, drawing, role play, games, and hands-on exercises with word cards and picture cards, in addition to traditional classroom activities. In any given class period, students are likely to work as a whole group, in pairs, in small groups, and (less often) alone. The majority of CROSSROADS exercises are appropriate for either close teacher supervision or independent work with peers.

What are the roles of the teacher in Crossroads?

Different activities in CROSSROADS call for different teacher roles, which might be identified as Community Developer, Director, Facilitator, Participant, Monitor, and Evaluator.

COMMUNITY DEVELOPER

If students are to become good communicators, they must be willing to take risks in English. One way you can encourage this is by establishing and maintaining a supportive learning community. Here are some ideas that may help you in your role as Community Developer:

- Use group-forming activities. Unit 1 of each level of CROSSROADS provides you with a group-forming activity that helps break the ice and gives students a chance to get to know each other. For each unit, the Teacher's Book includes suggestions for other group-forming activities, called warm-up activities, which can be used at any point in the class, and are an especially effective way to help new students feel comfortable.

- Encourage collaboration. With the Step-by-Step Teaching Procedures, pairs or groups work together to complete the exercise successfully. This means that each student has an investment in everyone else's progress.
- Make sure the same students do not always work together. If they do, students who are incompatible may feel "stuck," and those who are compatible may form cliques. Having students work with and get to know different students will help build and maintain a good learning environment.

DIRECTOR

Probably the most familiar role of the teacher is that of Director—the person who structures activities and makes clear what students are expected to do. As Director, you'll often be in the front of the room, leading the students through the exercises in the book. You will find that the Step-by-Step Teaching Procedures in the front of the Student Book, or the more detailed instructions in the Teacher's Book, will help you give the clear directions students need.

FACILITATOR

Most of the activities in CROSSROADS include a step where students work individually, in pairs, or in small groups. In these steps, the focus is away from the front of the room, and your role is to check on how the students are doing, and give help as needed.

In a paired or group activity, first give students a little time to find their partners and get settled. If students seem a little confused, refrain from stepping in too soon—a lot of real communication in English is probably going on while students sort things out. Do step in, however, if students seem frustrated.

Once students have settled into the activity, circulate unobtrusively, checking to see that they are doing what you intended. Help any students who seem confused about what the task is. After you're sure students understand the task, observe how well they're handling the content of the exercise. If a great number of students are having difficulty with a particular teaching point, stop the exercise and clarify the point.

While students are working, you may be called over by students who need help. Try to apportion your time evenly. If a few students need more attention, try putting them with peers who can help them, so that you remain available to others.

PARTICIPANT

Take part in communicative activities so that students can get to know you not only as the teacher, but also as a speaker of English. Your participation in pair or group work can provide students with a more challenging experience and you with valuable information about their progress. As an expert English speaker, you can add authentic gestures, reactions, and interjections to practice exercises, enriching students' experience of the language. This kind of participation is especially valuable in the culminating activity suggested in the *Memo to the Teacher* at the end of each unit.

MONITOR

Mistakes are an expected and even a valuable part of language learning. As Monitor, you provide students with feedback and correction so that they can learn from their mistakes. As Monitor, your first job is to help students recognize mistakes; your second job is to correct mistakes if students cannot self-correct or correct each other.

Keep in mind that students may be slow to grasp many distinctions that are obvious to you (for example, the need for the final *s* in third person singular, present tense verbs, or the fact that *he's* and *his* are not pronounced the same). Over-correction may discourage students so that they will not take risks. Your third job as Monitor, then, is not to avoid correcting too much.

Here are some specific suggestions for giving feedback and correction:

- Oral work: Say an incorrect word or phrase correctly when the student has finished but don't require the student to repeat after you.

In fact, the student may not be able to hear the correction at all, but other students may, and will be reassured if they too noticed the error.

- Written work at their seats: Carry a pad and pen with you while you circulate to see how students are doing. Help students correct themselves by pointing to mistakes on their papers. Give a student a chance to correct himself. If he doesn't recognize the mistake, write the word or phrase correctly on your pad and give the paper to the student. Stay long enough to be sure he is correcting the right thing.
- Written work at the board: In order to check written work students have done at their seats, send students with correct answers to write their sentences on the board. Some mistakes may appear in copying, so have the whole class scrutinize the sentences and suggest corrections. Either make the corrections yourself or have students make them. Then, one at a time, underline any mistakes that remain and wait for students to offer corrections. When students have corrected all they can, make the last corrections yourself.
  Have the whole class cooperate in a writing exercise, with one student writing at the board, but with all students responsible for the product. This means that students at their seats will be helping the writer at the board.
  Have a student write at the board, but set off a foot-wide margin at the board for yourself. If possible, both you and the student should have an eraser. When you see an error, write the word or phrase correctly on your section of the board. As soon as the student recognizes and corrects the error, erase what you've written, leaving only the student's writing on display.
- *Guess, What can you hear?, Practice,* and *What can you say?:* These recurring exercises encourage students to say what they think they see in a picture or hear in a conversation, and some of their suggestions will be "wrong." The point, however, is not just to come up with expected language, but also to involve students in the activity and allow them to try out new language.You can manage this dual purpose by simply accepting all guesses and repeating them in acceptable English—if necessary, changing the *form* of what the student has said, but not the *content.* However, if you are writing their guesses on the board, write only the responses you are looking for; or write them all, but erase the "wrong" ones before going on to the next step.
- Reading comprehension checks: A variety of exercise types check comprehension of reading on the Reading and Writing pages. Students work in pairs to answer specific questions about the reading. In these exercises (and in other written exercises where there is a single right answer), students should correct their mistakes. If you notice a wrong answer as you walk around while students are working, indicate the wrong answer. If they can't correct their own mistake, help them see the place in the reading where the answer can be found.

EVALUATOR

When you use the Progress Checks exercises to test students' performance of competencies, you are an Evaluator. You may prefer, however, to have students evaluate each other or themselves.

If you evaluate students' performance yourself, you'll need to occupy the other students with self-directed activities. Have students work together to "rehearse" while they are waiting their turns to be evaluated. Schedule the better-prepared students first. When they have been evaluated, they can tutor peers who need help. Students not needed as tutors can work on material from the *Multilevel Activity and Resource Package* or on material you have prepared.

If students evaluate each other, you may find it effective to have them evaluate and be evaluated by three different classmates. Two "passes" out of three would constitute a successful demonstration of competency. In this way, evaluation will not depend on a single student's judgment. Student Evaluators can initial each other's books or Individual Competency Checklists (pages 122–131) to certify demonstration of competency.

"BEFORE CLASS" ICON

The *Before Class* icon appears next to every exercise that requires preparation before class. "Preparation" could mean anything from planning an exercise or game to gathering the necessary materials for a task or exercise.

UNIT 1 Introductions

COMPETENCIES

Introduce yourself • Introduce others • Say where you are from • Say *Goodbye* • Fill in a simple form, including name, address, phone number, and area code • Ask someone to spell something • Spell something aloud • State your address, phone number, and area code • Write your country of origin • Write your first language

GRAMMAR

I'm, you're, he's, she's, we're, they're (review)
my, your, our, their, his, her (review)
I, you, we, they, he, she (review)

Warm-ups

BEFORE  CLASS

1. Where Are You From? (Use at any point in the unit.)
Tape a world map to a classroom wall. Have students write their names on cards. Shuffle them. Give each student a card with someone else's name on it. Have students find that person by asking, *Is your name* _________ *?* or *Is this your name? How do you say it?* When they find their partner, they ask *Where are you from?* Have students tape the cards around the perimeter of the map. Use string and pins to connect the names to the countries of origin. Encourage students to talk about their countries with a partner.

2. Introduction Chain (Use after page 4.)
To demonstrate, choose three students at random. Stand in a circle with them. Introduce yourself and the person on your left to the person on your right. That person then introduces himself and you to the person on *his* right. Have all the students stand in a circle and introduce themselves in this way until everyone has been introduced. For more of a challenge, have each person introduce more people. If the class is large, make several circles.

BEFORE  CLASS

3. Who Am I? (Use after page 6.)
Bring in pictures of several famous people who are still living. If possible, choose celebrities who come from your students' native countries. Write basic biographical information on the backs of the pictures. Include name, age, marital status, first language, native country, and city. Elicit questions about each person and write them on the board or OHP. Have a volunteer hold up a picture and use the information on the back to answer the other students' *yes/no* questions until they guess the person, or all the questions are answered.

Getting Started

1. GUESS. *(PAGE 1)*

Establishes the context of the unit.

Step-by-Step

1. Have students look at the pictures facing page 1 and point out Donna and Gloria. Have students identify Donna as the teacher and Gloria as a student. Then ask where Donna and Gloria are.
2. Ask students to guess what Donna and Gloria are saying. All responses are valid here. Respond to each guess by restating it in acceptable English.

2. WHAT CAN YOU HEAR?

Prepares students to read the first conversation on page 2.

Step-by-Step

1. Have students look at the picture while you play the tape or read the tapescript aloud.
2. Have students volunteer any words or sentences they can recall from the conversation. Acknowledge all contributions by restating them in acceptable English.
3. Let the students hear the conversation again to elicit more of it.

Conversations

1. PRACTICE. *(PAGE 2)*

Competency

[a] Introduce yourself.

Grammar

I'm, you're, he's, she's, we're, they're (review)

Step-by-Step

1. Play the tape or read the conversation aloud while students follow along in their books.
2. Elicit or demonstrate the meaning of *Glad to meet you* and *Glad to meet you, too*. Keep in mind that some students may not wish to shake hands because of different practices in their own culture. Let students know that *Hello* and *Hi* are functionally interchangeable, as well as *I'm* and *My name is....*
3. Have students repeat the conversation chorally sentence by sentence, and then practice in pairs.

2. TALK ABOUT YOURSELF.

Competency

[a] Introduce yourself.

Grammar

I'm, you're, he's, she's, we're, they're (review)

Vocabulary

Glad to meet you.

Step-by-Step

1. Write the conversation on the board or OHP, filling in the blanks with your name and the name of a volunteer.
2. Read the conversation aloud sentence by sentence and have students repeat. Have the volunteer say the conversation with you.
3. Erase the first two sentences and substitute them with *Hi*, your name, and the name of a volunteer. Have students repeat, then say the conversation with the volunteer.
4. Erase the names and have two more volunteers say the conversation for the class with both *Hi* and *Hello.*
5. Have students practice in pairs, changing partners and saying both parts.

Options

If your students are especially quiet or shy, in Step 3, have two volunteers come to the front of the class, facing each other. Stand behind each volunteer in turn, say her sentence, and have her repeat. Have two more volunteers repeat the process. Allow them to speak for themselves if possible, but stand behind each one as she speaks in case she needs help.

NOTE: In many Asian cultures, the usual order is family name first, then given name. Van Lee, for example, would be called Lee Van in his own language. Some Asian students may prefer to be called by their family name in class because their given name is used only among close friends. In the book Van Lee is called Van, but he might be called Lee or Mr. Lee.

In Spanish-speaking countries, an individual has two family names, the father's surname (for example, Rios) and mother's maiden name (for example, Ortega) making the person's last name Rios Ortega. Some Spanish speakers, especially in the United States, use only the first of their two last names. Married women use their father's first last name and their husband's first last name joined by the word *de* (of). For example, Ana Lopez de Rivera would be Mrs. Rivera in English.

3. PRACTICE.

Competency

[b] Introduce others.

Grammar

I'm, you're, he's, she's, we're, they're (review)

Step-by-Step

1. Give students time to look at the picture. Encourage them to guess or read what they can of the conversation.
2. Have students close their books. Play the tape or read the conversation. Use the picture of Gloria, Sue, and Van on page 1 of the Teacher's Book or stick figures to indicate which character is speaking each sentence.
3. Have students say anything they can recall of the conversation. Acknowledge all contributions by restating them in acceptable English.
4. Play the tape or read the conversation aloud while students follow along in their books. Then elicit or demonstrate the meaning of *friend* and *husband*. Refer to the picture on page 2, Exercise 3. (See page x of the Teacher's Book for suggestions on teaching vocabulary to low-level stu-

dents.) Tell students that *Nice* and *Glad* mean the same thing here. Play the tape as many times as students need.

5. Have the students repeat the conversation chorally sentence by sentence, and then practice in pairs.

NOTE: Gloria says *Nice to meet you* or *Glad to meet you* to Donna and Van because she doesn't know them. She says *Hi* to Sue because they are friends.

4. INTRODUCE TWO CLASSMATES.

Competency

b Introduce others.

Grammar

I'm, you're, he's, she's, we're, they're (review)

Step-by-Step

1. Write the conversation on the board or OHP with the names of two volunteers. Read it aloud and have students repeat.
2. Have a third volunteer introduce the first two volunteers to each other.
3. Have students practice in groups of three, changing partners and saying all the parts. Have several groups say the conversation for the class.

Cross-Reference

Multilevel Activity and Resource Package: Word Tap

Conversations

5. PRACTICE. *(PAGE 3)*

Competencies

a Introduce yourself.

b Introduce others.

c Say where you are from.

Grammar

I'm, you're, he's, she's, we're, they're (review)
my, your, our, their, his, her (review)

Step-by-Step

1. Give students time to look at the picture. Encourage them to guess or read what they can of the conversation.
2. Have students close their books. Play the tape or read the conversation. Use the pictures of Van and Antonio on page 1 of the Teacher's Book or stick figures to indicate which character is speaking each sentence.
3. Have students say anything they can recall of the conversation. Acknowledge all contributions by restating them in acceptable English.
4. Play the tape again while students follow along silently in their books. Then elicit or demonstrate the meaning of *wife, student,* and *That's nice.* Play the tape as many times as students need.
5. Have the students repeat the conversation chorally, and then practice in pairs.

Pronunciation

Use The Human Computer™ (see page xii) with *hi, hello, husband,* and *here*. Listen for the *h* at the beginning of these words which is produced by a slight constriction in the throat.

6. FOCUS ON GRAMMAR. REVIEW.

Grammar

I, you, we, they, he, she (review)
I'm, you're, he's, she's, we're, they're (review)
contractions (review)
my, your, our, their, his, her (review)

Step-by-Step

I, you, we, they, he, she

1. Write the six pronouns on the board. Use stick figures, yourself, and students to demonstrate meaning. Point to a pronoun and to people who exemplify it. Say the pronoun and have students repeat.

I'm, you're, he's, she's, we're, they're

2. Copy the left-hand box on the board or OHP. Point to each word as you read each sentence aloud and have students repeat.
3. Point to the missing pronouns on the board and have volunteers show you where to write them in the box *(You* and *we* with *are*; *he* with *is)*. Have students repeat the new sentences.

4. Have volunteers come to the board and write the six sentences from the box in their full form, using other countries if they wish. Correct any errors with the whole class and have students repeat the sentences and copy them.

contractions

5. Use the sentences on the board to elicit the contractions *'m*, *'s*, and *'re*. Show students that the apostrophe takes the place of missing letters. Have volunteers write the same sentences, with contractions, next to the sentences on the board. Again correct errors and have students repeat and copy.

my, your, our, their, his, her

6. Copy the right-hand box on the board or OHP. Point to each word in each sentence as you read it aloud and have students repeat.
7. Change *friend* to *friends*, elicit *are* and fill it in. Have students repeat the new sentences. Make sure they see that the change does not affect the possessive adjectives.

Option

BEFORE

CLASS

Use Word Cards from the *Multilevel Activity and Resource Package* or make your own cards. Let students work in groups of two or three to form sentences with the cards. They can also match items: *I am/I'm*, *She is/She's*, etc., and *I/my*, *she/her*, etc.

Going Further

BEFORE

CLASS

Set up a physical response drill. Write a sentence on the board, for example, *We're from Mexico.* Choose a volunteer from Mexico and have her bring together one or two other Mexican students, stand with them, and say the sentence. For *Their classmate is from Vietnam*, the volunteer brings together three other students, including one from Vietnam. She then says the sentence, pointing to the other two students on *Their* and to the Vietnamese student on *classmate.* If your students are all from the same country, give them large cards with the names of other countries. They can hold up the cards and role play.

NOTE: This is a good place to review other aspects of *be* in the present tense: negative statements *(She isn't from Mexico)*, *yes/no* questions *(Is she from Mexico?)*, *yes/no* short answers *(No, she isn't)*, and basic questions with *What* and *Where.*

7. TALK ABOUT THE STUDENTS.

Grammar

I'm, you're, he's, she's, we're, they're (review)
my, your, our, their, his her (review)

Step-by-Step

1. Write the conversation including the underlined sections on the board or OHP. Show students that *What's his name?* and *Where is he from?* come from the picture and cues.
2. Read the conversation sentence by sentence and have students repeat. Then read the other cues aloud one by one and have students repeat.
3. Have pairs of students say the conversation for the class until all the cues have been used. Then have students practice the conversation in pairs. They should change partners at least once, say both parts, and use all the cues.

Option

Use names and countries of students in your class. Write them on the board and have students practice before working in pairs. Have students point to the students they are talking about.

Going Further

Divide the class into teams to prepare as many statements *(She's...; She isn't...)* as they can about one of the team members or an imaginary person. Each member of the team says a sentence until all the prepared sentences have been used. The team with the most sentences wins.

Pronunciation

Use Minimal Pairs with *he's* and *his.* (See page xi.)

For the vowel of *he's,* the middle of the tongue is closer to the gum ridge, and is tenser, than for the vowel of *his.*

Cue	Response
he's	He's from Mexico.
his	His name is Antonio.

Conversations

8. TALK ABOUT YOURSELF. *(PAGE 4)*

Competency

[c] Say where you are from.

Grammar

I'm, you're, he's, she's, we're, they're (review)

Step-by-Step

1. Write the conversation on the board or OHP, filling in the blanks with your own information.
2. Read the conversation sentence by sentence and have students repeat. Then have a volunteer say the conversation with you.
3. Erase your information, exchange roles with the volunteer, write in the new information and demonstrate the conversation again.
4. Have students practice the conversation in pairs, changing roles once.

NOTE: This exercise provides the information students need in Exercise 9.

9. INTRODUCE YOUR PARTNER TO THE CLASS.

Grammar

I'm, you're, he's, she's, we're, they're (review)

Step-by-Step

1. Write Van's sentences on the board or OHP. Read them aloud and have students repeat. Erase *Gloria Rivas, She's,* and *El Salvador.* Fill in *Van Lee* and elicit the next sentence. Have students repeat.
2. Erase the information about Van and fill in the name and country of the student you interviewed in Exercise 8. Elicit *She's* or *He's*, fill it in, and have students repeat.
3. Have the student stand and introduce her to the class. Then have her introduce you.
4. Have students find their partners from Exercise 8 and give them a few minutes to prepare. Then have them introduce each other to the class.

10. PRACTICE.

Competency

[d] Say *Goodbye.*

Step-by-Step

1. Give students time to look at the picture in Exercise 11. Have students say what the people are doing. Then have them guess or read what they can of Sue and Gloria's conversation in Exercise 10.
2. Have students close their books. Play the tape or read the conversation aloud. Indicate which character is speaking.
3. Have students say anything they can recall of the conversation. Acknowledge all contributions by restating them in acceptable English.
4. Play the tape again while students follow along in the books. Play the tape as many times as students need.
5. Have students repeat the conversation and then practice in pairs.

NOTE: Students may ask about *Bye* and *See you.* You may want to convey that *Bye, Night,* and *See you* are shorter versions of *Goodbye, Goodnight,* and *I'll see you. Goodbye* and *Goodnight* are always appropriate. The other forms are often for family and friends.

Pronunciation

Use Minimal Pairs with *see* and *she.* (See page xi.) The /*s*/ vs. /*sh*/ contrast is particularly tricky before the vowel sound in these words, and especially for speakers of Japanese. Physically, the difference is that for /*s*/ the tongue is relatively tense, with a narrow rill or groove down the center where the air flow gets constricted and produces the noise. For /*sh*/ the tongue is less tense, and has a wider rill down the center.

Cue	**Response**
see	See you tomorrow.
she	She's my friend.

11. SAY GOODBYE.

Competency

[d] Say *Goodbye.*

Step-by-Step

1. Write the conversation in Exercise 11 on the board or OHP, using the names of four volunteers. Have the volunteers say the conversation for the class.
2. Demonstrate how friends wave goodbye. Have students practice. Have the volunteers say the conversation again, this time waving as they say goodbye.
3. Have students practice in groups of four, saying each part at least once.

Cross-Reference

Multilevel Activity and Resource Package: Grammar and Scrambled Sentences

Going Further

Introduce *Goodnight* and *Night*. See the note for Exercise 10.

Identify a relationship and have students decide how the people will say goodbye: a doctor and patient, a boss and employee, two good friends, and so on. Have volunteers role play each situation.

Paperwork

1. READ SUE'S ADDRESS BOOK. *(PAGE 5)*

Vocabulary on forms

area code, phone, address, apartment, city, state, ZIP code

Step-by-Step

1. Copy the blank address book page on the board or OHP.
2. Have volunteers say any words or phrases they can read or guess. As each word is said, write it on the address book page on the board, say it aloud, and have students repeat.
3. Elicit or supply missing items in the same way.
4. Elicit or demonstrate the meaning of the words on the address book page by asking questions about Antonio. *(What is Antonio's address?)*
5. Point to items on the completed address book page at random and have students read them aloud. Have students work in pairs, one saying a word and the other pointing.
6. Have students copy the words onto a separate piece of paper, practice writing each word several times, and then dictate the words to each other in pairs. Leave the page on the board.

2. WRITE YOUR ADDRESS AND PHONE NUMBER.

Competency

e Fill in a simple form, including name, address, phone number, and area code.

Step-by-Step

1. Fill in the page on the board with your own information using fictitious information if you wish. Then make statements with the information. *(My area code is 908.)*
2. Erase your information, interview a volunteer, and fill in the form again. Leave the filled-in form on the board for students to use as a model.
3. Have students fill in the form in their books with their information and check each other's answers in pairs.

NOTE: Students may want or need to give fictitious phone numbers and addresses. Show that this is acceptable by filling in the address book again, giving an obviously fictitious phone number (999-9999) and address (perhaps the school's address, if students know it) for yourself.

On the tape, building address numbers of up to four digits are grouped in two-digit sets, reading from the right. *810 Main St.* is *eight, ten*. *2267* is *twenty-two, sixty-seven*. However, *12780* is *one, two, seven, eight, oh*. Phone numbers are heard on the cassette in single digits with a pause after the third digit. *322-9671* is said *three two two, nine six seven one.* Area codes are also in single digits.

Cross-Reference

Multilevel Activity and Resource Package: Alphabet Game

3. PRACTICE.

Grammar

I'm, you're, he's, she's, we're, they're (review)
my, your, our, their, his, her (review)

Step-by-Step

1. Have students close their books. Play the tape or read the conversation aloud. Use the pictures of Sue and Antonio on page 1 of the Teacher's Book to indicate which character is speaking each sentence.
2. Have students say anything they can recall of the conversation. Acknowledge all contributions by restating them in acceptable English.
3. Play the tape again while students follow along silently in their books. Using the copy of Sue's address book on the board, elicit or demonstrate the meaning of *Antonio's first name, last name,* and *Could you spell his name please?* (See page x of the Teacher's Book for suggestions on teaching vocabulary to low-level students.) Play the tape as many times as students need.
4. Have students repeat the conversation chorally sentence by sentence, and then practice in pairs.

4. INTERVIEW THREE CLASSMATES.

Competency

f Ask someone to spell something.

g Spell something aloud.

h State your address, phone number, and area code.

Step-by-Step

1. Elicit the letters of the alphabet. As students say the letters, write them in order on the board or OHP. Have the students repeat.
2. Have students look at their names and addresses in Exercise 1. Have them silently practice spelling their names and addresses. Circulate and check pronunciation if students wish. Ask student "experts" to join you, circulating and correcting. Have volunteers spell their names or parts of their addresses for the class.
3. Elicit Sue's four questions from Exercise 3. Write them on the board and have students repeat them.
4. Have a volunteer speak for Antonio. Have another volunteer read the questions to "Antonio." Fill in the address book page on the board or OHP yourself.
5. Erase the information. Have a volunteer interview you and write your answers on the board. Correct the answers with the whole class.
6. Have students make an address book page on a separate piece of paper.
7. Have students ask and answer the questions with three classmates and fill in the address book page.

NOTE: Students may want or need to give fictitious phone numbers and addresses. Show that this is acceptable by repeating Step 5, giving an obviously fictitious phone number and address for yourself.

Option

In Step 4, demonstrate using clarification strategies by asking *Excuse me?* and *How do you spell that?* as students give information. Encourage students to use clarification strategies when needed in Step 6.

Cross-Reference

Multilevel Activity and Resource Package: Listening and Categories

Reading and Writing

1. WHAT CAN YOU SAY ABOUT YOUNG HO KIM? *(PAGE 6)*

Pre-reading.

Step-by-Step

1. Have students say any words or phrases from Young Ho Kim's student information card they can read or guess. As each word is said, write it on the board or OHP, say it, and have students repeat.
2. Elicit or supply missing items in the same way.
3. Elicit or demonstrate the meaning of words on the card by asking questions about Young Ho. *(Where does Young Ho go to school? What is his street address?)*
4. Point to items on the board at random and have students read them aloud.

2. READ ABOUT YOUNG HO.

Reading.

Step-by-Step

1. Give students a few minutes to look at the story and read what they can. Then play the tape or read the story aloud while students follow in their books.

2. Play the tape or read the story one sentence at a time and have students repeat. Then have volunteers read single sentences of the story aloud.

3. WRITE ABOUT YOUNG HO.

Comprehension check and writing.

Step-by-Step

1. Have a volunteer read aloud the first sentence in the reading (Exercise 2) and write it on one side of the board or OHP. Show students the example in Exercise 3 and write it next to the sentence on the board. Circle *my* and *his* to show students the changes.
2. Have students first work in pairs to do the entire exercise orally, then work alone to write it in their books.
3. Circulate while students are writing to give help. Send three students to the board to write their sentences under the ones with *his* and *he's*.
4. Have the writer of each sentence read her sentence aloud. After each sentence is read, have a volunteer read the corresponding sentence from Exercise 2. Correct any errors on the board with the whole class.
5. Have students check each other's papers from the board.

Going Further

Draw a female stick figure on the board or OHP and have students write about a woman student, So Young Kim. They will need to use *her* and *she*. Then have them write about Young Ho and So Young Kim (two stick figures), using plural forms *(their, they, names,* and *students)*.

4. WRITE YOUR STORY.
5. COPY YOUR STORY.

Competencies

[i] Write your country of origin.

[j] Write your first language.

Step-by-Step

1. Copy the passage on the board or OHP, leaving the blanks open.
2. Tell your own story to the class using Young Ho's story as a model. Fill in the blanks as you say the missing words. Also change *student* to *teacher* and rewrite the last sentence to read *I speak a little (French)*. Leave it on the board as a model.
3. Have students fill in the blanks in their books. Encourage them to help each other. Circulate to give help as needed or to listen to students' stories.
4. Have students work in pairs and tell their stories to each other. After one student talks, the other student restates the story to confirm understanding.
5. Have students copy their stories on a separate piece of paper. Encourage them to help each other. Circulate while students are writing to give help.

Going Further

Add a sentence to your story on the board. *(I like my job,* or *I teach English.)* Encourage students to extend their stories.

Cross-Reference

The New Oxford Picture Dictionary: Map of the World, pages 70–71

6. READ YOUR STORY TO YOUR GROUP.

Lets students share their writing.

Step-by-Step

1. Have a volunteer read her story aloud to the class. Lead the class in applause for the reader.
2. Have the class restate the story to confirm understanding. Encourage the volunteer to clarify meaning, if necessary.
3. Have students work in groups to read their stories in turn and to receive applause and responses from their peers.
4. Publish the stories by posting them in the classroom.

Going Further

Have a more advanced student makes a series of statements about someone in the class, or do this yourself. Students guess who is being described.

Cross-Reference

Multilevel Activity and Resource Package: Concentration, Board Game: Who Am I, and Game: High Card Wins

Reading and Writing

7. WHAT CAN YOU SAY ABOUT SUE'S CLASS? *(PAGE 7)*

Pre-reading.

Step-by-Step

1. Have students look at the pictures of Sue's class and say any words or sentences they can.
2. As each word, phrase, or sentence is suggested, write it on the board or OHP, say it, and have students repeat.
3. Elicit and add sentences with *there are*________, *men, women, different,* and *countries* if students have not used those words.
4. Point to items on the board at random and have students read them aloud.

8. READ ABOUT SUE'S CLASS.

Reading.

Step-by-Step

1. Review numbers by writing 0_ _ _ _ _ _ _ _ _ 10 on the board or OHP. Have students fill in the missing numbers. Have another volunteer write the spelled-out word underneath its corresponding number.
2. Point to the numbers and words and ask volunteers to say them. Then say the numbers and have volunteers point to the numbers and words.
3. Have students practice in pairs saying and pointing to the numbers and words. Each student should have a chance to both say and point to at least three numbers.
4. Give students time to look at the story and read what they can. Then, play the tape or read the story while students follow in their books.
5. Play the tape or read the story one sentence at a time and have students repeat chorally. Then have volunteers read sentences of the story aloud.

9. FILL IN THE CHART.

Comprehension check (Sue's class); pre-writing (Your class).

Step-by-Step

1. Copy the chart on the board or OHP, including the headings at the top and left side. Read the side headings one by one and have students repeat.
2. Elicit *ESL 2* for the first blank and fill it in. Have a volunteer read the corresponding sentence from Exercise 8. Have students point to the sentence in their books and repeat. Then have them fill in the first blank in their books.
3. In the same way, elicit and have students fill in the second blank. Then have them work in pairs to fill in the rest of the information about Sue's class.
4. Have volunteers fill in the answers on the board and check them with the whole class, comparing each answer with Exercise 8.
5. Show students that the next column is *Your Class.* Elicit the name of the class and the name of the school and fill them in.
6. Gather information and fill in the rest of the chart. Have several students count all the students, the men, and the women. When they agree on the numbers, have them fill in the chart. Then have students call out the names of their countries, spelling them if necessary. Have able students write the names on the board. Then have students count the number of different countries and fill in the chart. Do the same for their languages.

10. WRITE ABOUT YOUR CLASS.

Writing.

Step-by-Step

1. Copy the first sentence of the story in Exercise 8 on the board or OHP. Point to *ESL 2* and elicit the name of your class. Do the same with the name of the school. Have a volunteer say the new sentence and the other students repeat.
2. Have a volunteer write the new sentence on the board and have students copy it.
3. If necessary, do the same with the second sentence. Then have students complete the story about their class, working on their own papers, but helping each other. Circulate to answer questions and to check students' work.

4. Send students to the board to write sentences of the story. Correct any errors with the whole class and have students check their own work.

Cross-Reference

Multilevel Activity and Resource Package: Writing and Jigsaw Reading

Listening Plus

1. WHAT'S NEXT? *(PAGE 8)*

Predicting with social and grammatical clues.

Step-by-Step

1. With students' books closed, write the first response in *a (That's nice)* on the board or OHP. Read it aloud and have students repeat.
2. Have students work in pairs to imagine what might come before (for example, *I'm a new student. My wife is a new student, too.).*
3. Have pairs volunteer their ideas. Help the class evaluate each one.
4. Do the same with the other responses in *a* and leave them on the board.
5. Have students open their books and a volunteer come to the board.
6. Play the tape or read the tapescript aloud one conversation at a time. Have students point to the correct response in their books and have the volunteer point to it at the board. Play the tape as many times as students need.
7. Write *Yes, I am* (the first response in *b)* on the board or OHP. Read it aloud and have students repeat.
8. As in Step 2, have students imagine what might come before (for example, *Are you a new student?).* Help students see that the clues here are words like *you, he,* and *they,* unlike the social language clues in *a.*
9. Continue as above.

2. REVIEW...WRITE...NUMBER.

Focused listening.

NOTE: Students hear conversations beyond the level they are expected to produce. They need to understand only enough to complete the task.

ANSWER KEY

Write: b. *Russia, Russian;* c. *Egypt, Arabic;* d. *India, Hindi;* e. *Laos, Chinese*

Number: a. *4;* b. *2;* c. *5;* d. *3;* e. *1*

REVIEW.

Step-by-Step

1. Have students look at the illustrations and read or say anything they can about them.
2. As each item is volunteered, write it on the board or OHP, say it, and have students repeat.
3. Elicit any other vocabulary from the unit which appears in the illustrations.
4. Point to items on the board at random and have volunteers read them aloud.

WRITE.

Step-by-Step

1. Copy the answer blanks on the board or OHP.
2. Play the tape or read the first conversation aloud. Write the examples *(Canada, English)* on the board when students hear them. Show students that they are to fill in each person's country and first language.
3. Continue playing one conversation at a time and have students write their answers. Play the tape as many times as students need.
4. Have students compare their answers in pairs.
5. Play the tape again, one conversation at a time. Have a volunteer write the answers on the board. Correct the student's answers with the whole class.
6. Have students check their answers against the answers on the board, then play the tape once more so that students can verify their answers.

NUMBER.

Step-by-Step

1. Play the tape or read the tapescript aloud one conversation at a time, as many times as students need. Have students number the illustrations in the order of the conversations they hear.
2. Have students compare their answers in pairs.
3. Play the tape again and have a volunteer write the answers on the board. Correct any errors with the whole class.

4. Have students check their answers against the answers on the board, then play the tape once more so that students can verify their answers.

NOTE: *Number* has new conversations.

3. A, TELL ABOUT A PERSON IN 2...

Speaking and active listening.

Step-by-Step

1. Have a volunteer make statements about one of the people illustrated in Exercise 2. Repeat each statement. Demonstrate the use of confirmation strategies (for example, *Excuse me?).*
2. When the volunteer has finished, hold up your book and point to the person described.
3. Have another volunteer make statements about another of the people, and a third volunteer restate what is said and point to the person described.
4. Have students work in pairs to make statements and restate. Each student should change partners and describe all the people. Circulate to listen and give help as needed.

4. WHAT ABOUT YOU?

Listening and responding with personal information.

Step-by-Step

1. Play the tape once. Have students confer in groups to reconstruct the statement they heard. Circulate to hear what they say.
2. Repeat Step 1 until most groups have the gist of the statement.
3. Have groups share their reconstructions and help them reach a consensus.
4. Play the tape again so that students can verify their reconstruction.
5. Have students answer the question on the tape by writing similar information about themselves (for example, *I'm Alfredo Flores. I'm from Mexico.)*. Encourage students to extend their answers. *(I'm from Guadalajara, Jalisco, Mexico.)* Circulate to give help and feedback.
6. Have several volunteers put their answers on the board. Help the volunteers extend their answers if they have not already done so. Correct any errors with the whole class.
7. Have students compare their own answers with the answers on the board, then check each other's answers in pairs.

Cross-Reference

Multilevel Activity and Resource Package: Picture Story

Interactions

1. & 2. GET INFORMATION/GIVE INFORMATION *(PAGES 9 AND 10)*

Competencies

[f] Ask someone to spell something.

[g] Spell something aloud.

Vocabulary

box, book, clock, door, chalk, shelf, pencil, pen, notebook, chalkboard

Step-by-Step

1. Hold up actual classroom objects or pictures of them. Elicit the names, repeat them, and write them on the board or OHP. Point to each word and have a volunteer identify the object or picture by pointing to the picture or object and saying the name.
2. Ask volunteers to spell the words on the board. Leave the words on the board.
3. Write the conversation on the board or OHP.
4. Hold up your book and show students the two pages. Divide the class into a Student A group and a Student B group, and have them open their books to their group's page. Show them where Student A gets the questions and where B gets the answers.
5. Read the conversation aloud and have students repeat. Have a volunteer from each group say the conversation for the class.
6. To one side of the conversation, write *What's in Box E?* Elicit *door* from the B group and write it on the board. Say the question and answer and have students repeat in their groups.
7. Write *How do you spell that?* on the board. Elicit *D-O-O-R* and write it on the board. Say the question and answer and have students repeat.

8. Have a volunteer from each group come to the board and say the whole conversation with *door*. Have A write *door* on the board after B spells it for the second time.
9. Have A's and B's work in pairs to fill in the information. Each student should change partners and do both pages.

Cross-Reference

The New Oxford Picture Dictionary: A Classroom, page 76

Progress Checks

1. FILL IN THE FORM. *(PAGE 11)*

Competencies

[e] Fill in a simple form, including name, address, phone number, and area code.

[i] Write your country of origin.

[j] Write your first language.

In order to demonstrate the competency, the students must read the form and then fill it in. For this reason, the form is slightly different from other forms in the unit.

2. ASK QUESTIONS. FILL IN THE FORM.

Competency

[h] State your address, phone number, and area code.

The competency is demonstrated by giving the required information to a partner. It is not necessary to ask questions or to write in order to demonstrate this competency.

3. WHAT ARE THE PEOPLE SAYING?/ DO IT YOURSELF.

Competencies

[f] Ask someone to spell something.

[g] Spell something aloud.

Basic Conversation

A: *Write chalk.*
B: *How do you spell that?*
A: *C-H-A-L-K.*

Students tell each other what words to write and then spell them. Student A can choose any word she can spell.

Progress Checks

4. WHAT ARE THE PEOPLE SAYING?/ DO IT YOURSELF. *(PAGE 12)*

Competencies

[a] Introduce yourself.

[b] Introduce others.

[c] Say where you are from.

[d] Say *Goodbye.*

Basic Conversation

A: *Hello./Hi.*
I'm Frank/My name is Frank.
B: *Hello./Hi.*
I'm Lee./My name is Lee.

A: *Lee, this is Lynn. Lynn, this is Lee.*
B: *Glad/Nice to meet you.*
C: *Glad/Nice to meet you too.*

C: *Where are you from?*
B: *I'm from California.*

A: *Good night./Bye.*
B: *See you./See you Tuesday.*
Two students introduce themselves. Then one of them introduces a third student.

Memo to the Teacher

Option

Invite students from another class to come into your class. Have each of your students introduce herself to one of the guest students. Then have her introduce the guest to a classmate. Encourage students to extend their conversations as much as they can.

UNIT
2 Housing

COMPETENCIES

Ask about the number and types of rooms • Ask about rent and deposits • Find out about utilities • Identify basic types of housing • Identify the total due on monthly bills • Ask for information about locations of places in a neighborhood

GRAMMAR

simple present tense: affirmative and negative statements; *yes/no* questions; *yes/no* short answers (review)
but
across, down, on, around (location)

Warm-ups

1. Circle Rhythm Game (Use at any point in the unit.)
Make a set of cards with a month written in large letters on each card. Have students sit in circles of 12 or fewer and attach a card to their shirts with paper clips. Start rhythm clapping—patting your legs twice, clapping your hands twice, and snapping your fingers once left and once right. Then say your month on your left snap and a student's month on your right snap. That student continues by saying his month on the left snap and someone else's on the right. If he makes a mistake, he drops out, until there is just one person left.

2. Classroom Map (Use after page 18.)
Arrange desks, chairs, or rods to form blocks and streets. Use stacks of books to represent your school building. Have students stack books or rods to accurately represent the locations of other landmarks in the neighborhood, and then have them describe the place using prepositions of location. *(The bus stop is down the block.)* Ask *Where is the (___)?* and have other volunteers restate the locations.

3. I Have an Apartment (Use after page 16.)
With students' help, generate a word list of rooms, furniture, and appliances. List them on the board or OHP. Then have six students sit in a circle. The rest of the class observes and offers help by miming only. Take two items from the list on the board and say *My apartment has (a bedroom) and (a big closet).* Students continue adding items until everyone has added something. Then choose six more students. Continue until everyone has had a turn.

Getting Started

1. GUESS. *(PAGE 13)*

Establishes the context of the unit.

Step-by-Step

1. Have students look at the picture of Antonio, Elena, and the apartment manager, and ask where they are.
2. Have students identify Antonio and Elena as students and have them guess that the third person is the apartment manager. Ask students to guess what they are saying. All responses are valid here. Respond to each guess by restating it in acceptable English.

NOTE: In some apartment buildings there is only a landlord, not a manager. The manager is sometimes called the *building superintendent* or *super.*

2. WHAT CAN YOU HEAR?

Prepares students to read the first conversation on page 14.

Step-by-Step

1. Have students look at the picture while you play the tape or read the tapescript aloud.
2. Have students volunteer any words or sentences they can recall from the conversation. Acknowledge all contributions by restating them in acceptable English.
3. Let the students hear the conversation again to elicit more of it.

Conversations

1. PRACTICE. *(PAGE 14)*

Grammar

simple present tense: affirmative statements; *yes/no* questions (review)

Step-by-Step

1. Play the tape or read the conversation aloud while students follow along in their books.
2. Elicit or demonstrate the meaning of *apartment* and *Have a seat, please.*
3. Have students repeat the conversation sentence by sentence, and then practice in pairs.

2. TALK ABOUT YOURSELF.

Vocabulary

How do you do?

Step-by-Step

1. Write the conversation on the board or OHP filling in the blanks with the names of two volunteers.
2. Read the conversation aloud and have students repeat. Have the two volunteers say the conversation for the class.
3. Have students practice in pairs, changing partners, and saying both parts.

3. WHAT CAN YOU SAY?

Vocabulary

an apartment, a house, a furnished room

Step-by-Step

1. Ask students to look at the pictures and say any words they can read or guess. Use the board or OHP and write each type of housing as it is volunteered in a place corresponding to its location on the page. After you write each word, say it, and have students point to it in their books and repeat. Add any words students have not volunteered.
2. Ask a volunteer to stand and hold up the book for the class to see. (In large classes make smaller groups with a book held up in each.) Call on one volunteer to say a word and another to point to the picture for the class.
3. Have students work in pairs, one saying a word and the other pointing. Then have students write the words several times, and dictate them to each other in pairs.

Going Further

Have students add other types of housing they know. Show pictures illustrating ***a mobil home, a condominium, a townhouse,*** or ***a duplex*** (or use your regional equivalent of these terms).

Cross-Reference

The New Oxford Picture Dictionary: Houses, page 27; and The City, pages 44–45

4. PRACTICE.

Grammar

simple present tense: affirmative statements; *yes/no* questions; *yes/no* short answers (review)

Step-by-Step

1. Have students look at the floor plan. Encourage them to guess what Antonio, Elena, and Gina are saying now.
2. Have students close their books. Play the tape or read the conversation aloud. Use the OHP with the picture of Antonio and Elena on page 14 of the Teacher's Book and a stick figure for Gina to indicate which character is speaking each line.
3. Have students say anything they can recall of the conversation. Acknowledge all contributions by restating them in acceptable English.
4. Play the tape while students follow along in their books. Then elicit or demonstrate the meaning of *rent, bedroom, closets, kitchen, living room,* and *deposit.*
5. Have students repeat the conversation sentence by sentence, and practice in pairs.

NOTE: In some areas of the country, the first and last month's rent is collected and held as a deposit. In other areas, other amounts are collected. Discuss reasons why a deposit is requested (for repairs or cleaning when a tenant moves, for supplementing the landlord's income when a tenant breaks a lease, and so on).

Cross-References

The New Oxford Picture Dictionary: The Living Room, page 28; The Dining Room, page 29; The Kitchen, page 30; The Bedroom, page 32; and The Bathroom, page 34

Multilevel Activity and Resource Package: Picture Story

Conversations

5. TALK ABOUT ROOMS, RENTS, AND DEPOSITS. USE YOUR IMAGINATION. *(PAGE 15)*

Competencies

[a] Ask about the number and type of rooms.

[b] Ask about rent and deposits.

Step-by-Step

1. Review numbers and amounts of money by writing *$400, $450, $500, $550,* and so on up to *$1500* on the board or OHP. Say the amounts as you write them and have students repeat the numbers. Point to an amount and have a volunteer say it. Then review the names and functions of the rooms in the house by asking questions *(Where do you sleep?* or *Where do you eat?).*
2. Write the conversation on the board without filling in the handwritten parts. Show students that the information for the blanks comes from their imagination. Fill in the blanks as in the example.
3. Read the conversation aloud and have students repeat. Have pairs of students say the conversation for the class using different combinations of rooms, rent, and deposits.
4. Have students practice in pairs, changing partners, saying both parts, and using different rooms, rent, and deposits.

NOTE: On the cassette, *$1300* is *thirteen hundred dollars.*

6. WHAT CAN YOU SAY?

Vocabulary

water, gas, electricity, utilities

Step-by-Step

1. Ask students to look at the pictures and say any words they can read or guess. Use the board or OHP and write each word as it is volunteered in a place corresponding to its location on the page. After you write each word, say it, and have students point to it in their books and repeat. Add any words students have not volunteered.
2. Ask a volunteer to stand and hold up the book for the class to see. (In large classes, make smaller groups with a book held up in each.) Call on one volunteer to say a word and another to point to the picture.
3. Have students work in pairs, one saying a word and the other pointing. Then have students write each word several times and dictate the words to each other in pairs.

7. PRACTICE.

Competency

[c] Find out about utilities.

Step-by-Step

1. The conversation between Gina and Antonio continues. Have students close their books. Play the tape or read the conversation aloud. Use stick figures to indicate which character is speaking each line.
2. Have students say anything they can recall of the conversation. Acknowledge all contributions by restating them in acceptable English.
3. Play the tape while students follow along in their books. Play it as many times as students need.
4. Have students repeat the conversation sentence by sentence, and practice in pairs.

Pronunciation

Use Imitation and Correction (see page xi) with *has, what, gas, water, and,* and *deposit.* The tongue is far forward in the bottom of the mouth when making the vowel of *has, gas,* and *and.* The tongue is also low for the stressed vowwels of *what, water,* and *deposit,* but it is at the back of the mouth.

8. FOCUS ON GRAMMAR. REVIEW.

Grammar

simple present tense: affirmative and negative statements; *yes/no* questions; *yes/no* short answers (review)

Step-by-Step

simple present tense: affirmative statements

1. Write *They need an apartment* and *He needs an apartment* in two columns on the board or OHP. Read them and have students repeat.
2. Write *We need an apartment.* Elicit a corresponding sentence with *she,* write it in the appropriate column, read it, and have students repeat.
3. Continue with *I need an apartment.* Write it in the appropriate column and then elicit a corresponding sentence with *you.* Write it, read it, and have students repeat.

simple present tense: negative statements

4. Write *They don't need a big kitchen* and *He doesn't need a big kitchen* in two new columns. Read them and have students repeat.
5. Repeat Steps 2 and 3 with *We don't need a big kitchen/She doesn't need a big kitchen* and *I don't need a big kitchen/You don't need a big kitchen.*

simple present tense: *yes/no* questions; *yes/no* short answers

6. Write *Do they need two bedrooms?, Yes, they do,* and *No, they don't* in three columns. Elicit corresponding questions and answers using *we* and *you.*
7. Write *Does he need two bedrooms? Yes, he does,* and *No, he doesn't* in three more columns. Elicit corresponding questions and answers using *she* and *I.*
8. Have students work in pairs to say and write three more affirmative and negative sentences and three more questions and short answers using *have* and *want.* Have some students write their sentences on the board, correct them with the whole class, and have students copy them.

Option

Have students unscramble sentences to focus on the meaning and form of the simple present tense. Use Word Cards from the *Multilevel Activity and Resource Package* or make your own cards.

9. TALK ABOUT YOURSELF. USE THE WORDS IN 6.

Competency

C Find out about utilities.

Grammar

but

Step-by-Step

1. Write the conversation on the board or OHP without filling in the handwritten parts. Show students that the information for the blanks comes from Exercise 6. Fill in the blanks.
2. Elicit that *but* is used to contrast a positive statement with a negative. Show students that the positive or negative statement can come first. *(The rent includes water, but it doesn't include gas and electricity,* or *The rent doesn't include gas and electricity, but it includes water.)*
3. Read the conversation aloud and have students repeat. Also have them repeat the words in Exercise 6. Have pairs of students say the conversation for the class until all the words have been used.
4. Have students practice in pairs, changing partners, saying both parts, and using all the words in Exercise 6.

Conversations

10. WHAT CAN YOU SAY? *(PAGE 16)*

Vocabulary

drapes, carpeting, a stove, a refrigerator, a washer, a dryer

Step-by-Step

1. Ask students to look at the pictures and say any words they can read or guess. Use the board or OHP and write each word as it is volunteered in a place corresponding to its location on the page. After you write each word, say it, and have students point to it in their books and repeat. Add any words students have not volunteered.
2. Ask a volunteer to stand and hold up the book for the class to see. (In large classes, make

smaller groups with a book held up in each.) Call on one volunteer to say a word and another to point to the picture.

3. Have students work in pairs, one saying a word and the other pointing. Then have students write each word several times and dictate the words to each other in pairs.

11. PRACTICE.

Grammar

but

Step-by-Step

1. Elena, Gina, and Antonio's conversation continues. Ask students to close their books. Play the tape or read the conversation aloud, indicating which character is speaking each line.
2. Have students say anything they can recall of the conversation. Acknowledge all contributions by restating them in acceptable English.
3. Play the tape while students follow along in their books. Then elicit or demonstrate the meaning of *furnished, unfurnished,* and *laundry room.* Point out the pairs of positive and negative statements contrasted with *but.* Play the tape as many times as students need.
4. Have students repeat the conversation sentence by sentence, and practice in pairs.

Pronunciation

Use Imitation and Correction with *drapes, dryer.* (See page xi.) When making the /*dr-*/ sound, many students add a vowel between the /*d*/ and /*r*/, producing an extra syllable.

12. TALK ABOUT A HOUSE OR APARTMENT. USE THE WORDS IN 10.

Competency

[d] Identify basic types of housing.

Grammar

but

Step-by-Step

1. Write the conversation on the board or OHP without filling in the handwritten parts. Show students that the information for the blanks comes from Exercise 10. Fill in the blanks.
2. Read the conversation aloud and have students repeat. Also have them repeat the words in Exercise 10. Have pairs of students say the conversation until all the words have been used.
3. Have students practice in pairs, changing partners, saying both parts, and using all the words in Exercise 10.

Cross-Reference

Multilevel Activity and Resource Package: Scrambled Sentences, Listening, and Game: Word Search

Paperwork

1. READ AHMED'S UTILITY BILLS FOR SEPTEMBER. *(PAGE 17)*

Reading bills.

Step-by-Step

1. Draw an outline of the bills on the board or OHP.
2. Have volunteers say any words or phrases from the bills they can read or guess. As each word is said, write it on the bills on the board, say it aloud, and have students repeat.
3. Elicit or supply missing items in the same way.
4. Elicit or demonstrate the meaning of the words by asking questions about Ahmed's bills *(Who's Ahmed's gas company?* or *Where does Ahmed send his electric bill?).*
5. Point to items on the bills at random and have students read them aloud. Leave the bills on the board.

NOTE: Some of the vocabulary *(current, previous, billing date,* and *balance)* will be challenging for students. Elicit or supply simple definitions for these words.

In some parts of the country, gas and electric bills are combined and appear on the same bill.

Going Further

Bring in actual gas and electric bills to show students and have them locate various words and symbols.

2. HOW MUCH IS HIS GAS BILL THIS MONTH?...

Competency

[e] Identify the total due on monthly bills.

Step-by-Step

1. Write the names of the months on the board or OHP as students dictate them to you. Then write several dates on the board using numerals *(9/10* or *1/2)* and have students read the dates using ordinal numbers *(September 10th* or *January 2nd)*. Then write several dollar amounts on the board, have volunteers read them, say them again, and have students repeat *($41.32 is forty-one dollars and thirty-two cents,* or *forty-one thirty-two)*.
2. Use the bills on the board. Ask a volunteer to point to the total amount for each bill. Then have students point to the amount in their books.
3. Have a volunteer circle the amount for each bill, and then have students circle it in their books.

Option

Have students circle the totals on actual gas and electric bills.

Going Further

Bring in copies of other bills (newspaper, water, or telephone) and add other directions *(put a box around, check,* or *underline)*.

3. INTERVIEW THREE CLASSMATES.

Gives practice in speaking and writing.

Step-by-Step

1. Write the questions on the board or OHP, not filling in Ahmed's information yet.
2. Invite a student to speak for Ahmed. Interview "Ahmed" and write his answers with students' help.
3. Say the interview questions one at a time and have students repeat them.
4. Have a volunteer interview you and write your answers on the board. Correct the answers with the whole class.
5. Have students ask and answer the questions with three classmates and write their answers on a separate piece of paper.

NOTE: Have students give fictitious information if they don't know the answers to these questions or if they don't pay these bills.

Going Further

Have students add more interview questions *(How much is your rent?* or *What's the total for rent and utilities this month?)*.

Going Still Further

Make up math word problems based on the information gained in the interview *(If (Person A) earns $1,000 each month, how much money does he have left after paying rent and utilities?)*, or ask students to determine the average of all their utility bills.

Reading and Writing

1. THIS IS ANTONIO AND ELENA'S NEIGHBORHOOD... *(PAGE 18)*

Pre-reading vocabulary review.

Step-by-Step

1. Read each word in the list and have students repeat. Point to items at random and have students read them aloud.
2. Have students work in pairs to label the buildings on the map. Then have a volunteer stand and hold up the book for the class to see. Call on one volunteer to say the word and another to point to the building on the map. Have students check their answers and correct them if necessary.

2. WHAT CAN YOU SAY ABOUT THIS NEIGHBORHOOD?

Grammar

across, down, on, away, around (location)

Step-by-Step

1. On the board or OHP, copy the map without the prepositions. Have students look at the map and say anything they can about it. As each preposition of location is suggested, write it on the board or OHP, say it, and have students repeat.

2. Add any prepositions from the map that students have not volunteered. Point to items at random and have students read them aloud.
3. Have students look at the map in Exercise 1 and say anything they can about it using the prepositions of location. *(The apartment house is across the street from the school. The park is two blocks away. The bus stop is on the corner.)*

NOTE: The expression *on the next block* is used in some parts of the U.S., and *in the next block* in others.

Going Further

Have pairs of students ask and answer questions about the locations on the map. (A: *Where's the bus stop?* B: *It's around the corner from the supermarket).* Each student should change roles and use all the cues.

Cross-Reference

Multilevel Activity and Resource Package: Concentration, Sorting, and Grammar

Reading and Writing

3. READ ELENA'S LETTER TO HER FRIEND SANDY. *(PAGE 19)*

Reading.

Step-by-Step

1. Give students time to look at the letter and read what they can. Then play the tape or read the letter aloud while students follow in their books.
2. Play the tape one sentence at a time and have students repeat. Then have volunteers read sentences of the letter aloud.
3. As you read the letter or play the tape again, have students work in pairs, circling the places on the map as they hear them.

NOTE: Tell students that *dear* at the beginning of a letter means *hello.*

Option

Give simple definitions of *bedroom, living room,* and *kitchen* and have students point to these words in the letter.

4. DRAW A MAP OF YOUR NEIGHBORHOOD.

Pre-writing.

Step-by-Step

1. Draw a map of your neighborhood on the board or OHP, including as many locations in Exercise 1 as possible, and labelling them. Have students describe your map using prepositions of location. *(The park is across the street. The bus stop is two blocks away.)*
2. Have students draw maps of their own neighborhood and label them using the words in Exercise 1.
3. Have students ask and answer questions about their maps in pairs.

Option

If students prefer not to draw, give them Cuisenaire rods or other objects to represent their neighborhoods.

5. WRITE A LETTER ABOUT YOUR NEIGHBORHOOD.

Writing.

Step-by-Step

1. Tell the class about your own neighborhood, using Elena's letter in Exercise 3 as a model. Use the map of your neighborhood from Exercise 4 to illustrate your description. Point to each place on the map as you describe it. After each paragraph, help students restate what you have said to confirm their understanding. Then write your letter on the board or OHP. Begin with the date and *Dear* _____,. Leave it on the board for students to use as a model.
2. Have students work in pairs to describe their neighborhoods to each other, using the maps in Exercise 4. Then have them restate their partners' stories.
3. Have students write their letters on a separate piece of paper. Encourage students to help each other. Circulate to give help as needed or to listen to students' letters.

NOTE: Tell students to choose from several complimentary closes: *love* for close friends and relatives; and *regards, sincerely,* or *yours truly* for more distant friends or business acquaintances.

6. READ YOUR LETTER TO YOUR GROUP.

Lets students share their writing.

Step-by-Step

1. Have a volunteer read his letter aloud to the class. Then lead the class in applause for the reader.
2. Have him reread his letter one paragraph at a time. Have the class restate the letter to confirm understanding. Encourage the volunteer to clarify meaning, if necessary.
3. Have students work in groups to read their letters in turn, and to receive applause and responses from their peers.
4. Publish the letters by posting them in the classroom.

Cross-Reference

Multilevel Activity and Resource Package: Writing and Categories

Listening Plus

1. WHAT'S NEXT? *(PAGE 20)*

Predicting with social and grammatical clues.

Step-by-Step

1. Have students close their books. Write the first response for *a (How do you do?)* on the board or OHP. Read it aloud and have students repeat.
2. Have students work in pairs to imagine what might come before (for example, *This is Ms. Smith*).
3. Have pairs volunteer their ideas. Help the class evaluate each one.
4. Do the same with the other responses in *a*. Leave the responses on the board.
5. Have students open their books and have a volunteer come to the board.
6. Play the tape or read the tapescript aloud one conversation at a time. Have students point to the correct response in their books and have the volunteer point to it at the board. Play the tape as many times as students need.
7. Write *Yes, they do* (the first response in *b)* on the board or OHP. Read it aloud and have students repeat.
8. As in Step 2, have students imagine what might come before (for example, *Do they have a new house?)*. Help students see that the clues here are words like *they/their* and *I/my*, unlike the social language clues in *a*.
9. Continue as above.

2. REVIEW...WRITE...NUMBER.

Focused listening.

NOTE: Students hear conversations beyond the level they are expected to produce. They need to understand only enough to complete the task.

ANSWER KEY

Write: a. *rent $685.00, deposit $1,027.50;* b. *rent $540, deposit $300;* c. *rent $735, deposit $1,470;* d. *rent $625, deposit $937.50*

Number: a. *4;* b. *3;* c. *2;* d. *1*

REVIEW.

Step-by-Step

1. Have students look at the rooms and say anything they can about them. Acknowledge all contributions by restating them in acceptable English.
2. As vocabulary from the unit is volunteered, write it on the board or OHP, say it, and have students repeat.
3. Elicit any other vocabulary which will be helpful in distinguishing among the items.
4. Point to items on the board at random and have volunteers read them aloud.

WRITE.

Step-by-Step

1. Copy the answer blanks on the board or OHP.
2. Play the tape or read the first conversation aloud. Fill in the first rent and deposit as students hear it.
3. Continue playing the tape one conversation at a time and have students fill in the other answers. Play the tape as many times as students need.
4. Have students compare their answers in pairs.
5. Play the tape again, one conversation at a time. Have a volunteer write the answers on the board. Correct the student's answers with the whole class.
6. Have students check their answers against the answers on the board, then play the tape once more so that students can verify their answers.

NUMBER.

Step-by-Step

1. Play the tape or read the tapescript aloud one conversation at a time, as many times as students need. Have students number the rooms in the order of the conversations they hear.
2. Have students compare their answers in pairs.
3. Play the tape again and have a volunteer write the answers on the board. Correct any errors with the whole class.
4. Have students check their answers against the answers on the board, then play the tape once more so that students can verify their answers.

3. A, DESCRIBE AN APARTMENT IN 2...

Speaking and active listening.

Step-by-Step

1. Have volunteers make statements about one of the rooms in Exercise 2 (for example, *The kitchen is small. It has a stove and a refrigerator.)*. Repeat each statement. Demonstrate the use of clarification strategies (for example, *I'm sorry. Can you repeat that?)*.
2. Have students hold up their books and point to the room described.
3. Have students work in pairs to make statements, restate and point. Each student should change partners and describe all the rooms. Circulate to listen and give help as needed.

4. WHAT ABOUT YOU?

Listening and responding with personal information.

Step-by-Step

1. Play the tape once. Have students confer in groups to reconstruct the statement they heard. Circulate to hear what they say.
2. Repeat Step 1 until most groups have the gist of the statement.
3. Have groups share their reconstructions and help them reach a consensus.
4. Play the tape again so that students can verify their reconstruction.
5. Have students answer the question on the tape by writing similar information about themselves. Encourage students to vary or extend their answers. Circulate to give help and feedback.
6. Have several volunteers put their answers on the board. Help volunteers extend their answers if they have not already done so. Correct any errors with the whole class.
7. Have students compare their own answers with the answers on the board, then check each other's answers in pairs.

Interactions

1. & 2. GET INFORMATION/GIVE INFORMATION. *(PAGES 21 AND 22)*

Competency

f Ask for information about locations of places in a neighborhood.

Step-by-Step

BEFORE

CLASS

1. Write the conversation on the board or OHP. Review other neighborhood locations *(library, fire station, drugstore, post office, police station,* and *bank)* by asking students to name other buildings in the neighborhood they know. Write them, say them, and have students repeat. Elicit or supply simple definitions of these words, or hold up pictures of each building. Have one student say the word, and another point to the word on the board.
2. Divide the class into a Student A group and Student B group, and ask them to open their books to their group's page. Have the A group point to the missing information on their maps, and the B group point to their filled-in maps. Then have students switch roles for part 2.
3. Read the conversation aloud sentence by sentence and have students repeat. Have volunteers from both groups say the conversation. Erase it from the board. Call on new volunteers to say the conversation using the next cue *(bus stop)*. Show students how to fill in the information on the map.
4. Have students work in pairs to do the exercises. Each student should change partners and do both pages.

Cross-Reference

Multilevel Activity and Resource Package: Jigsaw Reading and Game: Build a Neighborhood

Progress Checks

1. WHAT ARE THE PEOPLE SAYING?/ DO IT YOURSELF. *(PAGE 23)*

Competencies

[d] Identify basic types of housing.

[b] Ask about rent and deposits.

[c] Find out about utilities.

[a] Ask about the number and types of rooms.

Basic Conversation

A: *Do you have an apartment for rent?*
B: *Yes, I do.*
A: *How many rooms does it have?*
B: *Three. A bedroom, a living room, and a kitchen.*
A: *What's the rent?*
B: *$650.*
A: *And what's the deposit?*
B: *$1300.*
A: *Does the rent include utilities?*
B: *Yes. It includes water, gas, and electricity.*

For *Do It Yourself,* have students ask about various types of apartments, rent, deposits, and utilities.

2. WHAT ARE THE PEOPLE SAYING?/ DO IT YOURSELF.

Competency

[f] Ask for information about locations of places in a neighborhood.

Basic Conversation

A: *Where's the supermarket?*
B: *It's on the next block.*

For *Do It Yourself,* have students ask for and give information about locations of places in their neighborhood. Have them use their maps from *Reading and Writing,* Exercise 4.

Progress Checks

3. CIRCLE THE TOTAL AMOUNT DUE. *(PAGE 24)*

Competency

[e] Identify the total due on monthly bills.

Have students circle the total amount due in all three bills and then check their answers in pairs.

Memo to the Teacher

Option

Invite an apartment manager to class, have another faculty member pose as one, or visit a nearby apartment complex. (Review questions students may ask beforehand with the apartment manager.) Have students ask about apartments in the manager's building—the number of rooms, the cost of rent and utilities, the deposit, and the location of places in the neighborhood. Divide students into groups and have each group keep a record of the answers for one apartment. Afterwards, have students compare the apartments.

UNIT

3 Community Services

COMPETENCIES	GRAMMAR
Fill out an application for a driver's license or ID • Fill out a money order • Correctly address an envelope including return address	*need to, have to, want to* simple past tense: affirmative and negative statements, *yes/no* questions, *yes/no* short and long answers, regular and irregular verbs

Warm-ups

1. Answers and Questions (Use at any point in the unit.)
Have students work in teams to generate a set of three questions and answers about members of the class (for example, *Where is Carlos from? Mexico.)* Then Team 1 gives Team 2 the first answer. If Team 2 can supply the correct question, they score 1 point. If Team 2 answers incorrectly, Team 1 gives the correct question and scores 1 point. Continue until all the questions have been used up. The team with the highest score wins.

2. Hangman (Use at any point in the unit.)
Choose a familiar word and draw blanks for each letter on the board or OHP. Draw a simple gallows next to the blanks. Each student has one chance to guess a letter. If the guess is correct, write the letter in the blank(s). If it's incorrect, draw one part of the hangman's body (head, neck, left arm, right arm, and so on) for each missed letter. The game ends when the word or the hanged man is complete. Continue with students supplying new words and drawing the hangman.

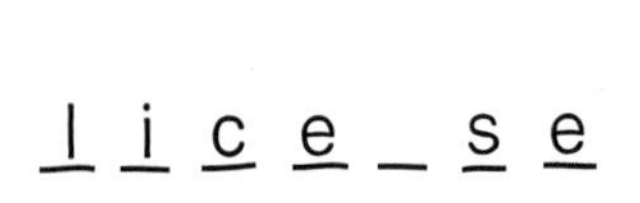

3. Guess My Height (Use after page 29.)
Have a volunteer stand at the front of the room. Each student asks the volunteer how tall he is. *(Are you 5 feet 8 inches tall?)* The person who guesses the volunteer's actual height wins. Repeat the guessing game with other volunteers. Bring a tape measure for verification.

Getting Started

1. GUESS. *(PAGE 25)*

Establishes the context of the unit.

Step-by-Step

1. Have students look at the pictures of Gloria, Sue and Van on page 25 of the Teacher's Book and point them out.
2. Give students time to look at the picture on page 25, then ask where Gloria, Sue, and Van are. Elicit the meaning of the *Department of Motor Vehicles* (the *DMV*).
3. Ask students to guess what Gloria, Sue, and Van are saying in the second picture. All responses are valid here. Respond to each guess by restating it in acceptable English.

2. WHAT CAN YOU HEAR?

Prepares students to read the first conversation on page 26.

Step-by-Step

1. Have students look at the pictures while you play the tape or read the tapescript.
2. Have students volunteer any words or sentences they can recall from the conversation. Acknowledge all contributions by restating them in acceptable English.
3. Let the students hear the conversation again to elicit more of it.

Conversations

1. PRACTICE. *(PAGE 26)*

Grammar

need to, have to, want to

Step-by-Step

1. Play the tape or read the conversation aloud while students follow along in their books.
2. Elicit or demonstrate the meaning of *get, take, road test, want to, have to, What about you?, need to,* and *good luck.* Use the pictures on pages 26 and 27 for *driver's license, learner's permit,* and *ID card.*
3. Have students repeat the conversation chorally sentence by sentence, and then practice in pairs.

Pronunciation

Use Minimal Pairs with *test* and *tests.* (See page xi.) Students from many language backgrounds will find the *-st* at the end of *test* challenging enough. The *-sts* at the end of *tests* may seem impossible. Students should try to imitate the native speaker who often uses a lengthened *s* at the end of *tests (tes-s)*. Cues and responses may be given by the teacher or by students.

Cue	Response
test	one test
tests	two tests

NOTE: In most states getting a driver's license involves passing a written test and an eye test in order to get a learner's permit, and then passing a road test to get the license itself.

It is possible to get an ID card from the Department of Motor Vehicles in most states.

2. WHAT CAN YOU SAY?

Vocabulary

written test, eye test, road test, ID card, change of address form, learner's permit

Step-by-Step

1. Ask students to look at the pictures and say any words they know. Use the board or OHP, and write each word as it is volunteered in a place corresponding to its location on the page. After you write each word, say it, have students point to the word in their books, and repeat. Then add any words students have not volunteered. *Take* is used with items pictured in the top row; *get* is used with items in the bottom row.
2. Ask a volunteer to stand and hold up the book for the class to see. (In large classes, make smaller groups with a book held up in each.) Call on one volunteer to say the word and another to point to the picture.
3. Have students work in pairs, one saying a word and the other pointing. Then have students write the words several times and dictate them to each other in pairs.

NOTE: The form of the eye test differs from state to state. Tell students what to expect in your state.

3. TALK ABOUT GOING TO THE DEPARTMENT OF MOTOR VEHICLES.

Grammar

have to, need to

Step-by-Step

1. Write the conversation on the board or OHP without filling in the handwritten parts. Use a student's name for the first blank. Show students that the words for the other two blanks come from Exercise 2 and fill them in. Remind students to use *take* with *tests.*
2. Read the conversation line by line and have students repeat, then do the same with the words in Exercise 2. Elicit *take* or *get* for each item. Have pairs of students say each item with *take* or *get* until all the words have been used. For example, *Take the eye test. Get an ID card.*
3. Have pairs of students say the conversation for the class with the other cues until all the words have been used. Then have them practice the conversation in pairs. Each student should change partners, say both parts, and use all the words.

Conversations

4. PRACTICE. *(PAGE 27)*

Grammar

simple past tense: *yes/no* questions, *yes/no* short and long answers

Step-by-Step

1. Give students time to look at the picture of Gloria and Van. Ask where Gloria and Van were in the last conversation. If students don't remember, have them turn to the picture on page 25. Encourage them to guess the conversation on page 27.
2. Have students close their books. Play the tape or read the conversation aloud. Use the picture of Gloria and Van on page 25 of the Teacher's Book. Point to indicate which character is speaking.
3. Have students say anything they can recall of the conversation. Acknowledge all contributions by restating them in acceptable English.
4. Play the tape or read the conversation while students follow along silently in their books. Then elicit or demonstrate the meaning of *pass, congratulations,* and *Oh, that's too bad.* (See page x of the Teacher's Book for suggestions on teaching vocabulary to low-level students.)
5. Have students repeat the conversation sentence by sentence, and then practice in pairs.

Pronunciation

Use The Human Computer™ or Imitation and Correction with *get, good, doing, did, buy,* and *bad.* (See page xii.) Listen for the */g/, /d/,* and */b/* at the beginning of these words. When making these sounds, the voice tract must be closed at one point or another. Either the voice box vibrates while it is closed or the vibration begins soon after the closure. In contrast, when making the */k/, /t/,* and */p/* sounds, which students frequently substitute for them, the voice box can start vibrating much later after the closure.

Many Spanish speakers have a tendency to make an initial */b/* into a */v/* sound. Vietnamese speakers find */g/* very difficult. Greeks may also have trouble with these sounds.

5. FOCUS ON GRAMMAR

Grammar

simple past tense: *yes/no* questions, *yes/no* short answers

Step-by-Step

yes/no questions

1. Copy the first sentence in the left-hand box on the board or OHP, leaving plenty of space between words so that you can create a substitution table on the board. Have students repeat the question.
2. Write *she* under *they,* elicit the full question, fill it in, and have students repeat.
3. Continue with *I, you, we, he, Gloria,* and *Kim and Lee.* Have students repeat each question. Leave the questions on the board.

yes/no short answers

4. Write *Yes, they did* and *No, they didn't* as two column heads to the right of the questions on the board or OHP. Again leave plenty of space between words.
5. Have a volunteer read the first question aloud, have another volunteer read the *yes* answer, and have all the students repeat. Then have another volunteer read the question again, have another read the *no* answer, and have all the students repeat.
6. Point to another question at random and have a volunteer read it. Elicit the two answers, fill them in, and have students repeat.
7. Continue until all the answers are filled in. Note that the question with *Gloria* is answered with *she,* and the question with *Kim and Lee* is answered with *they.*
8. Have students copy all the questions and answers from the board.
9. Have students work in pairs to generate orally and in writing other simple past tense *yes/no* questions with affirmative and negative short answers. Have students write their sentences on the board, correct any errors with the whole class, and have volunteers read the sentences from the board.

6. TALK ABOUT THE PEOPLE.

Grammar

simple past tense: *yes/no* questions, *yes/no* short answers

Step-by-Step

1. Write the conversation on the board or OHP without filling in the handwritten parts. Show students that the words for the first blank come from Exercise 4. Fill in the blank, read the question and have the students repeat. Elicit the answer and write it on the board. Read the conversation again and have students repeat.
2. Read the phrases aloud and have students repeat. Then ask the students *yes or no?* to check their understanding of each picture.
3. Have pairs of students say the conversation for the class until all the phrases have been used. Then have students practice the conversation in pairs. Each student should change partners, say both parts, and use all the phrases.

Conversations

7. PRACTICE. *(PAGE 28)*

Grammar

simple past tense: affirmative and negative statements

Step-by-Step

1. Give students time to look at the picture of Gloria and Sue. Encourage students to guess the conversation.
2. Have students close their books. Play the tape or read the conversation aloud. Use the pictures of Gloria and Sue on page 25 of the Teacher's Book to indicate which character is speaking each sentence.
3. Have students say anything they can recall of the conversation. Acknowledge all contributions by restating them in acceptable English.
4. Play the tape or read the conversation aloud while students follow along in their books. Then elicit or demonstrate the meaning of *not so good, happen,* and *glasses.* (See page x of the Teacher's Book for suggestions on teaching vocabulary to low-level students.)
5. Play the tape as many times as students need, then have them repeat the conversation sentence by sentence, and practice in pairs.

8. FOCUS ON GRAMMAR

Grammar

simple past tense: affirmative and negative statements with regular and irregular verbs

Step-by-Step

simple past tense: affirmative and negative statements with regular verbs

1. Copy the first box on the board or OHP, leaving plenty of space between words so that you can create a substitution table. Have students repeat each sentence.
2. Elicit a pronoun or a name for the first slot in the next sentence. Write it under *they,* elicit the affirmative sentence, write it, and have students repeat. Then do the same for the negative sentence.
3. Elicit two or three more sets with different singular and plural subjects.
4. Fill in *study* for the next sentence. Elicit the rest of the sentence, write it, and have students repeat. Then elicit the negative sentence.
5. Continue to fill out the substitution table using all three regular verbs.
6. Have students work in pairs to create and write other past tense sentences with the three regular verbs. Have volunteers put their sentences on the board, correct errors with the whole class, and have other volunteers read the sentences aloud.

simple past tense: affirmative and negative statements with irregular verbs

7. If possible, leave the first substitution table on the board while you begin another with the first sentence from the right-hand box.
8. Build the second table in the same way, eliciting as much as possible from the students, and having them repeat each sentence.
9. Have students copy all the sentences from the board.
10. Have students create and write other past tense sentences with the three irregular verbs. Have volunteers put their sentences on the board, correct any errors with the whole class, and have other volunteers read the sentences aloud.

Pronunciation

Use Imitation and Correction with regular simple past tense verbs: *passed, studied,* and *needed.* (See page xi.) Tell students to listen for the pronunication of *-ed* which sounds like */t/* after verbs ending in a voiceless sound (like *pass)*, like */d/* after verbs ending in a voiced sound (like *study)*, and like */id/* after verbs ending with either *d* or *t (need, want).*

9. TALK ABOUT THE PEOPLE.

Grammar

simple past tense: affirmative and negative statements

Step-by-Step

1. Write the conversation on the board or OHP without filling in the handwritten parts. Show students the words for the first blank come from *a* and fill it in. Read the question and have students repeat. Elicit the answer for the second blank. If students give a short answer, elicit *No, she didn't pass the road test.* Write the answer in the second blank.
2. Read the conversation aloud sentence by sentence and have students repeat. Then do the same with the cues. After you read each cue, ask students *yes or no?* to check their understanding of each picture.
3. Have students practice the conversation in pairs. Each student should change partners, say both parts, and use all the cues.

Paperwork

1. READ GLORIA'S APPLICATION. *(PAGE 29)*

Vocabulary on forms

print, first name, middle name, last name, full name, mailing address, ZIP code, sex, male (m), female (f), height, weight, date of birth

Step-by-Step

1. Draw an outline of the application form on the board or OHP.
2. Have volunteers say any words or phrases from the form in the book they can read or guess. As each word is said, write it on the form on the board, say it aloud, and have students repeat.
3. Elicit or supply missing items in the same way.
4. Elicit or demonstrate the meaning of the words on the form by asking questions about Gloria. *(What is Gloria's full name?)* Introduce the two-letter abbreviations for states. Hand out a list of state abbreviations for reference if available.

5. Point to items in the completed form at random and have students read them aloud. Leave the form on the board.

2. FILL IN THE APPLICATION.

Competency

[a] Fill out an application for a driver's license or ID.

Step-by-Step

1. Write the hair and eye colors on the board. Say them and have students repeat. Show students the picture of Gloria and ask them about her hair and eye color. Have them find the answers in Exercise 1. Ask them about your own hair and eye color and circle the correct answer. Do the same with volunteers. If your students all have the same coloring, bring in pictures showing hair and eye colors different from theirs.
2. Use the form on the board. Erase Gloria's information and fill in the form one blank at a time with information about yourself. Make statements with the information.
3. Erase your information, interview a volunteer and fill in the form. Review ordinal numbers for street names *(17th Street)*. Leave the filled-in form on the board for students to use as a model.
4. Have students fill in the forms in their books with their own information. Bring a scale and tape measure for students to weigh and measure themselves. Provide assistance when necessary. Have students check each other's answers in pairs.

NOTE: Students may want or need to give fictitious information at several points on this form. Show that this is acceptable by repeating Step 2, giving obviously fictitious information about yourself.

Going Further

Have students fill out some actual forms: the registration form used by your school, a voter registration form, and so on.

3. INTERVIEW THREE CLASSMATES.

Gives practice in speaking and writing.

Step-by-Step

1. Write the question on the board or OHP, not filling in Gloria's information yet.
2. Invite a student to speak for Gloria. Interview "Gloria" and write the answers with students' help.
3. Say the interview questions one at a time and have students repeat them.
4. Have a volunteer interview you and write your answers on the board. Correct the answers with the whole class.
5. Have students ask and answer the questions with three classmates and write their answers on a separate piece of paper.

Cross-Reference

Multilevel Activity and Resource Package: Listening

Guess heights - p. 26

Reading and Writing

1. WHAT CAN YOU SAY ABOUT ANTONIO? *(PAGE 30)*

Grammar

simple past tense: regular and irregular verbs

Step-by-Step

1. Have students look at the three pictures. Point to the first picture and ask *Where did Antonio go?* Have students answer using *went.* Repeat each sentence in acceptable English and write it on the board. Do the same with the other verbs/ pictures and have students copy the sentences under the appropriate pictures in their books.
2. Read the sentences from the board one at a time and have students repeat. Point to the sentences at random and have volunteers read them aloud.

Cross-Reference

The New Oxford Picture Dictionary: The U.S. Postal System, page 46

Pronunciation

Use Minimal Pairs with *send* and *sent* to practice the contrast between /*d*/ and /*t*/. (See page xi.)

Cue	**Response**
send	Send it today.
sent	I sent it yesterday.

2. READ ABOUT ANTONIO.

Reading.

Step-by-Step

1. Give students a few minutes to look at the story and read what they can. Then play the tape or read the story aloud while students follow silently in their books.
2. Play the tape or read the story one sentence at a time and have students repeat it chorally. Then have volunteers read single sentences of the story aloud.

NOTE: Antonio had to buy two postal money orders because the maximum dollar amount for one money order is $700 and his deposit was $1300.

Going Further

Rewrite the story changing it to the simple present tense. Students start by writing *Every month Antonio needs a money order for the rent for his apartment.* They must change *money orders* and *receipts* to the singular form.

3. NUMBER THE SENTENCES IN ORDER.

Comprehension check.

Step-by-Step

1. Read the sentences and have students repeat.
2. Show students that the first sentence is numbered *1.* Have students repeat it. Have a volunteer find the same information in Exercise 2 and read it aloud *(He went to the post office...).* Have the other students point to the sentence in Exercise 2 and repeat.
3. Have a volunteer give the second sentence in Exercise 3 and have students repeat. As in Step 2, have students identify the corresponding part of the reading in Exercise 2.

4. Have students work in pairs to number the sentences in order. Circulate to answer questions.
5. Check answers by having volunteers read the sentences in order. Have each volunteer identify the corresponding part of the reading in Exercise 2.
6. Have students copy the sentences in order on a separate piece of paper.

Cross-Reference

Multilevel Activity and Resource Package: Concentration 1, Grammar, and Picture Story

Going Further

Make up a new story with the same verbs. Write the sentences on separate strips of paper. Give each small group a set of strips. Have students put the strips in order and read the story aloud.

Reading and Writing

4. SEND THIS MONEY ORDER TO BARBARA DAY. *(PAGE 31)*

Competency

[b] Fill out a money order.

Step-by-Step

1. Copy the money order on the board or OHP without the names and addresses.
2. Have students look at the money order and read aloud anything they can.
3. Fill in the order with your name and address under *purchaser*. Write *Barbara Day* under *pay to* and point to the instructions in the Student Book or ask volunteers to supply the address. As they say it, write it on the form in the *pay to* section.
4. Ask questions about the information to check students' understanding. For example, ask who the purchaser is, what *pay to* means, who Barbara Day is, and what the money order is for. Leave the form on the board for students to use as a model.
5. Have students fill in the forms in their books and check each other's work in pairs.

Competency

[c] Correctly address an envelope including return address.

Step-by-Step

1. Draw a blank envelope on the board or OHP. Refer students to the picture of Antonio's envelope in Exercise 1, page 30 for the correct form.
2. Elicit Barbara Day's name, elicit the address, and write the information on the envelope.
3. Write your return address in the upper left corner. Ask questions about the information on the envelope to check students' understanding. Leave the filled-in envelope on the board as a model.
4. Have students fill in the envelopes in their books. Pair students to check each other's work.

NOTE: Students may want or need to give a fictitious address. Show that this is acceptable by giving an obviously fictitious address for yourself in Step 3.

Options

Have students address real envelopes to you and each other. Have students address mailing labels for packages or large envelopes.

5. WRITE ABOUT YOURSELF.

Grammar

simple past tense: regular and irregular verbs

Step-by-Step

1. Have students close their books. Point to the money order and envelope on the board as you tell the story in Exercise 5.
2. Help students restate what you have said to confirm their understanding.
3. Have students open their books. Copy the story on the board, not filling in the missing words. Fill in the first blank. Show students that the words for the blanks come from Exercise 1, page 30. Have volunteers tell you the missing verb and write it in the blank. Read each sentence aloud, and have students repeat. Leave the story on the board as a model.
4. Have students work in pairs filling in the blanks in their books. Circulate to answer questions and check students' work.

6. COPY YOUR STORY ON A SEPARATE PIECE OF PAPER.

Writing.

Step-by-Step

1. Have students copy their stories on a separate piece of paper. Circulate to see that students are copying accurately. Have them add one more sentence to the story and check their work with a classmate.
2. Have several students read their stories to the class. Then publish the stories by posting them in the classroom.

Cross-Reference

Multilevel Activity and Resource Package: Writing, Jigsaw Reading, and Go Fish

Option

Select words students should learn how to spell: *money order, apartment,* and *receipt,* as well as the verbs *bought, sent, kept,* and so on. Erase these words in the passage on the board and have volunteers fill them in. Correct the passage with the class. Have volunteers choose two or three words to erase and have other students fill them in.

Listening Plus

1. WHAT'S NEXT? *(PAGE 32)*

Predicting with social and grammatical clues.

Step-by-Step

1. Have students close their books. Write the first response in *a (Congratulations)* on the board or OHP. Read it aloud and have students repeat.
2. Have students work in pairs to imagine what might come before (for example, *Did you pass your road test? Yes, I did*).
3. Have pairs volunteer their ideas. Help the class evaluate each one.
4. Do the same with the other responses in *a* and leave the responses on the board.
5. Have students open their books and have a volunteer come to the board.
6. Play the tape or read the tapescript aloud one conversation at a time. Have students point to the correct response in their books and have the volunteer point to it at the board. Play the tape as many times as students need.
7. Write *Yes, they did* (the first response in *b)* on the board or OHP. Read it aloud and have students repeat.
8. As in Step 2, have students imagine what might come before (for example, *Did they pass their road tests?)*. Help students see that the clues here are words like *they/their, she/her,* and *he/his,* unlike the social language clues in *a*.
9. Continue as above.

2. REVIEW...WRITE...NUMBER.

Focused listening.

NOTE: Students hear conversations beyond the level they are expected to produce. They need understand only enough to complete the task.

ANSWER KEY

Write: a. *222 S. Wilson St., Apt. 202, Mule Creek, NM 88051*; b. *1660 W. Main St., Apt. H, Fox Lake, IL 60020*; c. *1595 Utah Blvd. N., Iowa City, IA 52240*; d. *222 E. Adams St., Hartford, CT 06112*

Number: a. *3;* b. *4* ; c. *1;* d. *2*

REVIEW.

Step-by-Step

1. Have students look at the envelopes and money orders and read or say anything they can about them.
2. As vocabulary from the unit is volunteered, write it on the board or OHP, say it, and have students repeat.
3. Elicit any other vocabulary which will be helpful in distinguishing the four documents.
4. Point to items on the board at random and have volunteers read them aloud.

WRITE.

Step-by-Step

1. Copy the addresses and answer blanks on the board or OHP.
2. Play the tape or read the first conversation aloud. Fill in the blanks in the first address as students hear it.

3. Continue playing one conversation at a time and have students fill in the other addresses. Play the tape as many times as students need.
4. Have students compare their answers in pairs.
5. Play the tape again, one conversation at a time. Have a volunteer write the answers on the board. Correct the student's answers with the whole class.
6. Have students check their answers against the answers on the board, then play the tape once more so that students can verify their answers.

NUMBER.

Step-by-Step

1. Play the tape or read the tapescript aloud one conversation at a time, as many times as students need. Have students number the documents in the order of the conversations they hear.
2. Have students compare their answers in pairs.
3. Play the tape again and have a volunteer write the answers on the board. Correct any errors with the whole class.
4. Have students check their answers against the answers on the board, then play the tape once more so that students can verify their answers.

3. A, TELL ABOUT A PICTURE IN 2...

Speaking and active listening.

Step-by-Step

1. Have a volunteer make statements about one of the documents illustrated in Exercise 2 *(It's to Ms. Marta Lopez, It has a stamp,* etc.). Repeat each statement. Demonstrate the use of clarification strategies (for example, *I'm sorry. How do you spell that?)* if pronunciation is not clear.
2. When the volunteer has finished, hold up your book and point to the document described.
3. Have another volunteer make statements about another of the documents, and a third volunteer restate what is said and point to the document described.
4. Have students work in pairs to make statements and restate. Each student should change partners and describe all the documents. Circulate to listen and give help as needed.

4. WHAT ABOUT YOU?

Listening and responding with personal information.

Step-by-Step

1. Play the tape once. Have students confer in groups to reconstruct the statement they heard. Circulate to hear what they say.
2. Repeat Step 1 until most groups have the gist of the statement.
3. Have groups share their reconstructions and help them reach a consensus.
4. Play the tape again so that students can verify their reconstruction.
5. Have students answer the question on the tape by writing similar information about themselves. Encourage students to vary or extend their answers *(I live in Chicago, Illinois now. I live in an apartment. It's on Elm Street)*. Circulate to give help and feedback.
6. Have several volunteers put their answers on the board. Help the volunteers extend their answers if they have not already done so. Correct any errors with the whole class.
7. Have students compare their own answers with the answers on the board, then check each other's answers in pairs.

Cross-Reference

Multilevel Activity and Resource Package: Concentration 2 and Sequencing

Interactions

1. & 2. GET INFORMATION/GIVE INFORMATION. *(PAGES 33 AND 34)*

Information gap for communicative practice.

Step-by-Step

1. Write the conversation on the board or OHP. Review the vocabulary on the forms.
2. Hold up your book and show students these two pages. Divide the class into a Student A group and a Student B group, and have them open their books to their group's page. Show them where Student A asks questions and where B gets the answers to A's questions. Use the

example *(Manuel)* to show students that A asks about the blanks on her page and that B has the answers.

3. Read the conversation aloud and have students repeat. Have a volunteer from each group say the conversation for the class.
4. To one side of the conversation write *What________height?* Elicit the whole question and write it on the board. Say the question and have students repeat.
5. Write *What color__________ eyes?* Elicit the whole question and write it on the board. Say the question and have students repeat.
6. Have A's and B's work in pairs to fill in the information. Each student should change partners and do both pages.

Cross-Reference

Multilevel Activity and Resource Package: Categories, Game: Who is Pat Brown?, and Scrambled Sentences

Progress Checks

See page viii for suggestions on using Progress Checks.

1. FILL OUT THE MONEY ORDER. *(PAGE 35)*

Competency

[b] Fill out a money order.

Students should use their own name and address for *purchaser* and any name or address for *pay to.*

2. ADDRESS THE ENVELOPE FOR THE MONEY ORDER.

Competency

[c] Correctly address an envelope including return address.

Students should use the same names and addresses as in Exercise 1.

Progress Checks

3. FILL OUT THE APPLICATION. *(PAGE 36)*

Competency

[a] Fill out an application for a driver's license or ID.

To protect their privacy, students may have used fictitious information when they filled out forms on page 29. They need to understand that true information must be given on official forms outside of class. The competency is really demonstrated only by using true information.

Memo to the Teacher

Option

Take students to the Department of Motor Vehicles in your community. Have them observe people applying for their licenses and taking the tests, as well as the people working there. When they come back to class, have volunteers describe what they saw. Repeat each sentence in acceptable English and write it on one side of the board or OHP. Read the sentences aloud and have students repeat. Have students decide on the best order for the sentences. Write them in order on the other side of the board. Have students copy the story on a separate piece of paper. Post the story in the classroom.

UNIT
4 School

COMPETENCIES

State the number of years of previous education and study of English • Fill out a form, including birthplace, date of arrival in the U.S., number of years of previous education, and number of years of study of English • Give dates, including date of arrival in the U.S.• Fill out a form, including names, relationships, and ages of family members

GRAMMAR

simple past tense: *wh-* questions
last week/month/year; weeks/months/years ago
in, on, for (time)

Warm-ups

1. Strip Story (Use at any time during the unit.)
Make up seven-sentence stories using the past tense and a specific chronological order. Cut the story into sentence strips. Form groups of seven and give one strip to each student to memorize without showing it to the others. Then collect the strips and have groups figure out the correct order of the sentences. When they are ready, have each group line up in order and tell their story to the rest of the class.

2. Family Tree (Use after page 38.)
Students work in small groups to create a fictitious family. Each student writes one family member's name on a card and assumes that identity. The family holds up their name cards and answers questions from the rest of the class about their relationships or related subjects.

3. Time Line (Use after page 42.)
Write a year on the board and say something you did that year. The next person says what you did and adds one thing that he did, and so on. *(I got married in 1979; Ms. Jones got married, and I arrived in the U.S. in 1979; and Ms. Jones got married, José arrived in the U.S., and I finished high school in 1979.)*

Getting Started

1. GUESS. *(PAGE 37)*

Establishes the context of the unit.

Step-by-Step

1. Have students look at the picture and point out Olga, Yuri, and Ray. Ask where the characters are.
2. Refer students to the picture facing page 1 in their books, so that they can see Olga is a student.
3. Ask students to guess what Olga, Yuri, and Ray are saying. All responses are valid here. Respond to each guess by restating it in acceptable English.

2. WHAT CAN YOU HEAR?

Prepares students to read the first conversation on page 38.

Step-by-Step

1. Have students look at the picture while you play the tape or read the conversation aloud.
2. Have students volunteer any words or sentences they can recall from the conversation. Acknowledge all contributions by restating them in acceptable English.
3. Let the students hear the conversation again to elicit more of it.

Conversations

1. PRACTICE *(PAGE 38)*

Vocabulary

May I help you?, grandmother, enroll, Sure

Step-by-Step

1. Play the tape or read the conversation aloud while students follow along in their books.
2. Elicit or demonstrate the meaning of *May I help you?, enroll, grandmother,* and *Sure.* Use the family tree in Exercise 2 or refer to the picture on page 37.
3. Have students repeat the conversation chorally, sentence by sentence, and then practice in pairs.

2. WHAT CAN YOU SAY?

Vocabulary

grandmother, grandfather, grandparents, aunt, uncle, mother, father, parents, brother, sister

Step-by-Step

1. Ask students to look at the Horowitz family tree, and say any words they know. Use the board or OHP and write each word as it is volunteered in a place corresponding to its location on the page. Include names and family relationships. Pronounce each word after you write it and have students point to the word in their books and repeat. Then add any words students have not volunteered.
2. Ask a volunteer to stand and hold up the book for the class to see. (In larger classes, make smaller groups with a book held up in each group.) Call on one volunteer to say a word and another to point to the picture for the class.
3. Have students work in pairs, one saying a word and the other pointing. Then have students write each word several times, and dictate the words to each other in pairs.

NOTE: Students need to know that, generally speaking, *family* in the United States means one couple and their children. A family tree like the one on page 38 includes people related by blood or marriage. *Family* may be defined differently in your students' cultures.

3. TALK ABOUT YURI'S FAMILY.

Vocabulary

Family relationships

Step-by-Step

1. Write the conversation on the board or OHP without filling in the handwritten parts. Show students that the information for the first blank comes from Exercise 2. Fill in the first and second blanks with *Olga.*
2. Elicit *Olga is Yuri's grandmother* and fill in the blank. Read the conversation sentence by sentence and have students repeat. In the same way, read Yuri's relatives' names and relationships and have students repeat.
3. Elicit plural forms by asking *Who are Olga and Boris?* Repeat Step 2 with the plurals *Elena and Mikhail/Yuri's parents; Nataly and Vladimir/Yuri's aunt and uncle;* and *Ivan and Anna/Yuri's brother and sister.*
4. Have pairs of students say the conversation for the class until all the names and family relationships have been used. Then have students practice the conversation in pairs, changing partners, saying both parts, and using all the names and relationships.

Going Further

Choose another person in the family tree, Natalya for example, and repeat the conversation from her point of view. *(Who is Vladimir? He is Natalya's husband.)* Introduce *son, daughter, children, grandson, granddaughter, grandchildren, husband, wife, niece,* and *nephew.*

Expand the family tree by adding children to Elena and Mikhail's branch. Introduce *cousin.*

Cross-Reference

The New Oxford Picture Dictionary: People and Relationships, page 2; and The Family, page 3.

4. DRAW YOUR FAMILY... TALK ABOUT YOUR FAMILY.

Vocabulary

Family relationships

Step-by-Step

1. Draw a picture of you and your family (not your family tree) using stick figures on the board or OHP. Write the conversation next to it without filling in the handwritten part.
2. Elicit the question *Who's that?* from a volunteer, then write the question and your answer on the board. Read the conversation and have students repeat it. Then say the conversation with a volunteer.
3. Erase the information and repeat Step 2 with another family member. Continue in this way until all the figures have been discussed.
4. Have students draw their own pictures and practice the conversation in pairs until all the figures have been discussed.

Going Further

Have students write names under the figures in their pictures. Have them ask and answer any questions they can *(Who's Mary? Is she a student? What does she do?)*.

Conversations

5. PRACTICE. *(PAGE 39)*

Grammar

simple past tense: *wh-* questions
in, on (time)

Step-by-Step

1. Give students time to look at the picture of Ray, Olga, and Yuri.
2. Have students close their books while you play the tape or read the conversation aloud. Use stick figures to indicate which character is speaking.
3. Have students say anything they can recall of the conversation. Acknowledge all contributions by restating them in acceptable English.
4. Play the tape again while students follow along in their books. Then elicit or demonstrate the meaning of *When did you come to the United States? Where did you study English?* and *in 1990, on May 20, 1990, last year*
5. Play the tape as many times as students need, then have them repeat the conversation sentence by sentence, and practice in groups of three.

Pronunciation

Use Imitation and Correction with *very* and *well.* (See page xi.) Students from many parts of the world have trouble with the consonants at the beginning of these words. For most, the harder one is */w-/*, made by rounding the lips. The */v-/*, in contrast, involves putting the lower lip against the upper teeth so that turbulence develops as the breath emerges.

6. FOCUS ON GRAMMAR.

Grammar

simple past tense: *wh-* questions

Step-by-Step

1. Have one volunteer read *Where did they study English?*, and another read *They studied in New York.* Write the sentences side by side on the board or OHP. Read them and have students repeat.
2. Draw a line under *Where* and *in New York.* Elicit or show students that a *where* question asks about a place *(New York)*.
3. Repeat Steps 1 and 2, eliciting more *where* questions and answers. Show students that *in* is used with cities, states, and countries.
4. Repeat Steps 1 and 2 for *When did he enroll here?* and *He enrolled here on May 20, 1990.* Elicit more *when* questions and answers. Elicit or show students that a *when* question asks about time *(on May 20, 1990)*.

Option

Have students create questions and answers with Word Cards from the *Multilevel Activity and Resource Package* to help learn the sentence patterns.

7. TALK ABOUT THE PEOPLE.

Grammar

simple past tense: *wh-* questions
in, on (time)

Step-by-Step

1. Write the conversation on the board or OHP. Show students that *When did he come here?* and *He came here on June 3, 1989* come from the picture and cues.
2. Read the conversation sentence by sentence and have students repeat. Then read the other cues aloud one by one and have students repeat.

3. Have pairs of students say the conversation for the class until all the cues have been used. Then have students practice the conversation in pairs. They should change partners at least once, say both parts, and use all the cues.

Conversations

8. PRACTICE. *(PAGE 40)*

Grammar

simple past tense: *wh-* questions

Step-by-Step

1. Refer students to the picture of Ray, Olga, and Yuri in Exercise 5, page 39. Then have students close their books. Play the tape or read the conversation, indicating which character is speaking each line.
2. Have students say anything they can recall of the conversation. Acknowledge all contributions by restating them in acceptable English.
3. Play the tape or read the conversation aloud while students follow along in their books. Then elicit or demonstrate the meaning of *three months ago*, *for six months*, and *for nine years*.
4. Have the students repeat the conversation sentence by sentence, and then practice in pairs.

NOTE: Although Olga might not like to say how long she studied, she must give this information for school records. In a social conversation, however, Olga could answer *I'd rather not say.*

Pronunciation

Use Imitation and Correction with *school, speak,* and *study.* (See page xi.) Students from Spanish and South Asian backgrounds tend to put a vowel at the beginning of words that start with /s/ plus another consonant.

9. FOCUS ON GRAMMAR.

Grammar

simple past tense: *wh-* questions
in, on, for (time)
last week/month/year; weeks/months/years ago

Step-by-Step

last week/month/year; weeks/months/ years ago

1. Make two columns on the board or OHP. Have a volunteer read *When did you come to California?* and write it in the left column. Have another volunteer read *Three weeks ago* and write it in the right column. Read the two items aloud and have students repeat.
2. Write *When did you take your eye test?* in the left column and have students repeat. Point to the right column. Elicit an answer with *ago,* write it, and have students repeat. Elicit or show students that *ago* is used with *weeks, months,* or *years.*
3. Point to the right column again, elicit an answer with *last,* and write it. Then elicit a corresponding question and write it in the left column. Elicit or show students that *last* is used with *week, month,* or *year.*

in, on **(time)**

4. Write short answers with *in* and *on* in the right column and elicit corresponding questions for the left column. Elicit or show students that *in* is used with years and months and *on* with days and dates. Have students copy them.

simple past tense: *wh-* questions
for **(time)**

5. Write *How long did you live in New York?* and *For ten years* on the board or OHP. Elicit several examples for each column. Show students that *for* is used with amounts of time and answers the question *how long.*
6. Write *when* and *how long* in two columns. Have volunteers write the appropriate time phrase under each column to check their understanding.

Options

Write phrases of place and time on the board, point to them at random, and have students produce an appropriate *when, where,* or *how long* question. Ask questions using *how long* and *when* and have students answer in complete sentences.

10. TALK ABOUT OLGA.

Grammar

simple past tense: *wh-* questions
in, on, for (time)
last week/ month/year; weeks/months/years ago

Step-by-Step

1. Write the conversation on the board or OHP, not filling in the handwritten parts. Show students that *When/come to the U.S.?* comes from Exercise 5 and fill in the blanks. Follow the same procedure with the answer.
2. Read the conversation sentence by sentence and have students repeat. Then read the other cues aloud one by one and have students repeat.
3. Have pairs of students say the conversation for the class until all the cues have been used. Then have students practice the conversation in pairs. They should change partners at least once, say both parts, and use all the cues.

11. TALK ABOUT YOURSELF.

Competency

[a] State the number of years of previous education and study of English.

Grammar

simple past tense: *-wh* questions
in, on, for (time)
last week/month/year; weeks/months/years ago

Step-by-Step

1. Use the conversation on the board for Exercise 10, replacing Olga's name with *you, she* with *I*, and ... *came to the U.S. in May 1990* with a blank. Fill in the blank with a volunteer's answer.
2. Read the conversation line by line and have students repeat. Then have the volunteer say the conversation with you.
3. Show students that the information for the questions comes from Exercise 10. Erase the filled-in sections and replace with new information about another volunteer. Have pairs of volunteers say the conversation for the class. Continue with other volunteers and information until all the cues have been used. Then have students practice the conversation in pairs, changing partners, saying both parts, and using all the cues.

NOTE: Students may want or need to give fictitious information about themselves. Show that this is acceptable by repeating Step 2 giving obviously fictitious information about a volunteer.

Cross-Reference

Multilevel Activity and Resource Package: Scrambled Sentences, Picture Story, and Grammar

Going Further

Expand the conversation by encouraging students to ask other questions. *(How long did you work in Panama?* or *What did you study in the Dominican Republic?)* Have volunteers write the new questions on the board.

Paperwork

1. READ OLGA'S ENROLLMENT FORM. *(PAGE 41)*

Vocabulary on forms

Mr., Ms., Mrs., Miss, mo. (month), marital status, single, married, separated, widowed, date of birth, birthplace, date of arrival in U.S., in case of emergency, notify, relationship

Step-by-Step

1. Draw an outline of the enrollment form on the board or OHP. Have students look at the form in their books and say any words and phrases they can.
2. As each word or phrase is suggested, write it on the board or OHP. Say the item and have students repeat it.
3. Add any words or phrases from the form that students have not volunteered. Say the item and have students repeat it.
4. Point to items on the board at random and have volunteers read them aloud.
5. Ask questions to check students' comprehension of the content of the form. Call on volunteers to answer.
6. Have students work in pairs to ask and answer comprehension questions about the form.

2. FILL IN THE FORM.

Competency

[b] Fill out a form, including birthplace, date of arrival in the U.S., number of years of previous education, and number of years of study of English.

Step-by-Step

1. Copy the form on the board or OHP or use the form from Exercise 1. Fill it in one blank at a time with information about someone else, and then make a statement with the information. *(In case of emergency, call Gloria Lopez. She's Jim's wife.)* Then elicit a question and answer from two volunteers.
2. Erase the information. Have students interview a volunteer and fill in the form again. Have students make statements about the volunteer. Leave the filled-in form on the board for students to use as a model.
3. Have students fill in the form in their books with their information and check each other's answers in pairs.

Going Further

Have students work in pairs, asking and answering questions based on the information in their enrollment forms.

3. INTERVIEW THREE CLASSMATES.

Competency

C Gives dates, including date of arrival in the U.S.

Step-by-Step

1. Copy the questions on the board, not filling in Olga's information.
2. Invite a student to speak for Olga. Interview "Olga" and write her answers with students' help.
3. Say the interview questions one at a time and have students repeat.
4. Have a volunteer interview you and write your answers on the board. Correct the answers with the whole class.
5. Have students ask and answer the questions with three classmates and write their answers on a separate piece of paper.

Option

Have students ask and answer other questions based on the form.

Cross-Reference

Multilevel Activity and Resource Package: Listening and Peer Dictation/Dates

Reading and Writing

1. WHAT CAN YOU SAY ABOUT RAMONA AND HER FAMILY? *(PAGE 42)*

Pre-reading.

Step-by-Step

1. Have students look at the time line and read anything they can. Write each suggestion on the board. Say *I was born on September 1, 1950* and have students repeat.
2. Elicit phrases or sentences that students have not volunteered.
3. Point to items on the board at random and have students read them aloud.

NOTE: Students may ask about *had* in *I had my first child.* Ramona *has* three children. They *were born* in 1970, 1972, and 1974.

2. READ ABOUT RAMONA AND HER FAMILY.

Reading.

Step-by-Step

1. Give students time to look at the story and read what they can. Then play the tape or read the story aloud while student follow in their books.
2. Play the tape or read the story one sentence at a time and have students repeat chorally. Then have volunteers read sentences of the story aloud.

3. ANSWER THE QUESTIONS...

Comprehension check.

Step-by-Step

1. Write the question *When was Ramona born?* on the board or OHP. Elicit the answer *Ramona was born on September 1, 1950* and write it next to the question.
2. Have students work in pairs to answer the questions.
3. Write the questions on the board as volunteers read them. Have volunteers write the answers on the board next to each question. Have the class correct the sentences on the board if necessary. Have students check their work.

Pronunciation

Use The Human Computer™ with the questions and answers. (See page xii.)

Going Further

Have students rewrite Ramona's story from Exercise 2, page 42, changing *I* to *She* and making other appropriate changes.

Reading and Writing

4. FILL IN THE FORM. *(PAGE 43)*

Competency

d Fill out a form, including names, relationships, and ages of family members.

Step-by-Step

1. Copy the blank form on the board or OHP.
2. Draw a picture of your family using stick figures as you did in Exercise 4, page 38. Fill in the form one blank at a time with information about a member of your family. Teach the meaning of *relationship.* Make a statement with the information. *(My sister's name is Jean.)*
3. Erase your information, interview a volunteer, and fill in the form. Leave the filled-in form on the board for students to use as a model.
4. Have students fill in the form in their books with their own information. Have students share information about their families with a partner by making statements based on the form.

5. WRITE A TIME LINE FOR YOURSELF AND YOUR FAMILY.

Pre-writing.

Step-by-Step

1. Have students look at Ramona's time line on page 42. Draw a line across the upper part of the board and write four or five dates above it for yourself and your family.
2. Point to the first date and say *What happened in (year)?* Answer the question. Write the answer on the board under the date with a line connecting the two. Then have students repeat the question *What happened?* several times. Point to the next date and have students ask *What happened in (year)?* After giving your answer, write it on the board under the date with a line connecting the two.
3. Ask students *What happened in (year)?* and have them answer with *You (Your)....*
4. Erase your information. Have a volunteer write four or five dates and repeat Steps 2 and 3.
5. Have students complete the time lines in their books and share this information with a partner.

Going Further

Rather than drawing a flat time line, show students how to draw one with "mountains" for the high points and "valleys" for the low points in their lives. Give them an opportunity to express their feelings about these events.

6. WRITE ABOUT YOURSELF.

Writing.

Step-by-Step

1. Tell your own story to the class, using Ramona's story as a model. After each paragraph, help students restate what you have said to confirm their understanding. Then write the paragraph on the board or OHP. Leave it on the board for students to use as a model. Have students note how your story differs from Ramona's (maybe there are grandchildren; maybe no one died).
2. Have a volunteer tell his story to the class. Write his sentences on the board as a model.
3. Have students work in pairs to tell their stories and restate their partners' stories.
4. Have students write their stories. Circulate to give help as needed or to listen to their stories, and encourage them to help each other.

Option

Have students cut their stories into sentence strips. Have students in groups of three or four exchange sets of strips. Have each student arrange a set of strips in order and write the sentences in a paragraph.

7. READ YOUR STORY TO YOUR GROUP.

Lets students share their writing.

Step-by-Step

1. Have a volunteer read his story aloud to the class. Then lead the class in applause for the reader.
2. Have him reread his story one paragraph at a time. Have the class restate the story to confirm understanding. Encourage the volunteer to clarify meaning, if necessary.
3. Have students work in groups to read their stories in turn and to receive applause and responses from their peers.
4. Publish the stories by posting them in the classroom.

Cross-Reference

Multilevel Activity and Resource Package: Writing, Strip Story, and Categories

Listening Plus

1. WHAT'S NEXT? *(PAGE 44)*

Predicting with social and grammatical clues.

Step-by-Step

1. Have students close their books. Write the first response in *a* on the board or OHP. Read it aloud and have students repeat.
2. Have students work in pairs to imagine what might come before.
3. Have pairs volunteer their ideas. Help the class evaluate each one.
4. Do the same with the other responses in *a* and leave the responses on the board.
5. Have students open their books and a volunteer come to the board.
6. Play the tape or read the tapescript aloud one conversation at a time. Have students point to the correct response in their books and have the volunteer point to it at the board. Play the tape as many times as students need.
7. Repeat the process for *b*.

Listening Plus

2. REVIEW...WRITE...NUMBER.

Focused listening.

ANSWER KEY

Write: a. *3/22/30;* b. *10/15/57;* c. *9/1/50;* d. *12/26/46;* e. *9/24/70;* f. *12/1/72;* g. *7/27/74*

Number: a. *5;* b. *4;* c. *7;* d. *1;* e. *3;* f. *6;* g. *2*

REVIEW.

Step-by-Step

1. Have students look at the family tree and read or say anything they can about the people.
2. As vocabulary from the unit is volunteered, write it on the board or OHP, say it, and have students repeat.
3. Elicit any other vocabulary which will be helpful in distinguishing among the people.
4. Point to items on the board at random and have volunteers read them aloud.

WRITE.

Step-by-Step

1. Copy the answer blanks on the board or OHP.
2. Play the tape or read the first conversation aloud. Fill in the first date of birth *(3/22/30)* as students hear it.
3. Continue playing one conversation at a time and have students fill in the other dates of birth. Play the tape as many times as students need.
4. Have students compare their answers in pairs.
5. Play the tape again, one conversation at a time. Have a volunteer write the answers on the board. Correct the student's answers with the whole class.
6. Have students check their answers against the answers on the board, then play the tape once more so that students can verify their answers.

NUMBER.

Step-by-Step

1. Play the tape or read the tapescript aloud one conversation at a time, as many times as students need. Have students number the pictures in the order of the conversations they hear.

2. Have students compare their answers in pairs.
3. Play the tape again and have a volunteer write the answers on the board. Correct any errors with the whole class.
4. Have students check their answers against the answers on the board, then play the tape once more so that students can verify their answers.

3. A, TELL ABOUT THE PEOPLE IN 2.

Speaking and active listening.

Step-by-Step

1. Have volunteers make statements about one of the people in Exercise 2. Repeat each statement. Demonstrate the use of clarification strategies (for example, *Did you say December 26?)*.
2. Have students hold up their books and point to the person described.
3. Have students work in pairs to make statements, restate, and point. Each student should change partners and describe all the people. Circulate to listen and give help as needed.

4. WHAT ABOUT YOU?

Listening and responding with personal information.

Step-by-Step

1. Play the tape once. Have students confer in groups to reconstruct the statement they heard. Circulate to hear what they say.
2. Repeat Step 1 until most groups have the gist of the statement.
3. Have groups share their reconstructions and help them reach a consensus.
4. Play the tape again so that students can verify their reconstruction.
5. Have students answer the question on the tape by writing similar information about themselves. Encourage students to vary or extend their answers. Circulate to give help and feedback.
6. Have several volunteers put their answers on the board. Help the volunteers extend their answers if they have not already done so. Correct any errors with the whole class.
7. Have students compare their own answers with the answers on the board, then check each other's answers in pairs.

Cross-Reference

Multilevel Activity and Resource Package: Sentence Generation

Interactions

1. & 2. GET INFORMATION/GIVE INFORMATION. *(PAGES 45 AND 46)*

Information gap for communicative practice.

Step-by-Step

1. Review the vocabulary on forms by having students ask questions about Olga's enrollment form on page 41. *(How old is Olga? When did she arrive in the U.S.?)* Then write the conversation on the board or OHP.
2. Divide the class into a Student A group and a Student B group and have them open their books to their group's page. Have the A group point to the items they need to fill in Ovidio's form, and B's point to the filled-in items on their page. Then have students switch roles for Sumi's form, Exercise 2.
3. Read the conversation aloud sentence by sentence and have students repeat. Teach *When was Ovidio born?* as a formula rather than as a new verb tense and *Did you say...?* and *That's right* as a new clarification strategy. Take B's part and have a volunteer take A's part. Suggest that Student A say *I'm sorry. What did you say?* if they did not catch all of the information. Demonstrate that Student B should repeat the information if Student A did not understand.
4. Have volunteers from both groups say the conversation. Erase it from the board. Call on new volunteers to say the conversation using the next piece of missing information. Write their conversation on the board or OHP.
5. Have students work in pairs to fill in their forms. Each student should change partners and do both pages. Have students check their answers by comparing them with the filled in version in the book.

Cross-Reference

Multilevel Activity and Resource Package: Concentration and Board Game: In the Past

Progress Checks

See page viii for suggestions on using the Progress Checks.

1. FILL OUT THE FORM. *(PAGE 47)*

Competency

[b] Fill out a form, including birthplace, date of arrival in the U.S., number of years of previous education, and number of years of study of English.

2. FILL OUT THE FORM.

Competency

[d] Fill out a form, including names, relationships, and ages of family members.

Progress Checks

3. WHAT ARE THE PEOPLE SAYING?/ DO IT YOURSELF. *(PAGE 48)*

Competencies

[a] State the number of years of previous education and study of English.

[c] Give dates, including date of arrival in the U.S.

Basic Conversation

A: *Where are you from?*
B: *I'm from Mexico.*
A: *How long did you go to school in Mexico?*
B: *I went to school there for six years.*
A: *How long did you study English?*
B: *I didn't study English.*
A: *When did you arrive in the United States?*
B: *On June 1, 1982.*
A: *When did you enroll in your adult school?*
B: *Four months ago.*

In *Do It Yourself,* to demonstrate competency, have students work in pairs to say the conversation using their own information. If it is helpful, they can fill in the blanks in the bubbles. Although the questions are not required for competency attainment for this unit, students should be able to form the questions. Encourage them to use time phrases with *last, for, ago, in,* and *on* in their answers. Have some of the students act out the conversation for the class.

Memo to the Teacher

Option

Invite your school registrar, or guests who are willing to play the role, to come to one of your class sessions. Have the registrar interview small groups of students and fill in actual enrollment forms for your school. Encourage students to ask for clarification if they do not understand the guest's questions.

UNIT

5 Health

COMPETENCIES	GRAMMAR
Identify common injuries • Ask about medical treatment • Identify common health problems and treatment • Read the names of common medicines • Read and follow instructions on medicine labels • Follow simple instructions for medical treatment • Repeat instructions to check your understanding	future tense with *be + going to*: affirmative and negative statements, *yes/no* questions, *wh-* questions imperatives (review) *next week, tomorrow, in fifteen minutes*

Warm-ups

BEFORE  CLASS

1. Vocabulary Brainstorm (Use at the beginning of the unit.)
Show students a picture illustrating a health-related vocabulary item *(body, medicine, injury)*. Have students call out words they associate with the picture. Write their words on the board. Have students work in small groups to write sentences using the words. Have groups share their work with the class.

2. Do As I Say (Use at any point in the unit.)
Give commands. *(Put your hands on your knees. Put your thumb on your nose.)* At first, give the command and demonstrate the action. Then, just give the command. Have volunteers give commands to other students. Play the game in small groups or with the entire class.

3. I Don't Know (Use after page 51.)
Write this dialogue on the board or OHP:

A: *What is (Student C) going to do next Saturday?*
B: *I don't know. What are* **you** *going to do next Saturday?*
C: *I* ______________.
B: *She* ___________.

Demonstrate the conversation with two volunteers. Take B's part. Have A ask you the first question. say your line and coach C to answer the question. Then report C's answer to A. Have students work in groups of three. Have students play all three roles.

Getting Started

1. GUESS. *(PAGE 49)*

Establishes the context of the unit.

Step-by-Step

1. Have students look at the pictures of Ahmed's accident, then ask where the characters are.
2. Ask students what is happening to Ahmed in the first picture.
3. Have students identify Ahmed as a student and guess that Betty is a co-worker and Joe is the store manager. Ask students to guess what Betty and Joe are saying. All responses are valid here. Respond to each guess by restating it in acceptable English.

2. WHAT CAN YOU HEAR?

Prepares students to read the first conversation on page 50.

Step-by-Step

1. Have students look at the pictures while you play the tape or read the tapescript aloud.
2. Have students volunteer any words or sentences they can recall from the conversation. Acknowledge all contributions by restating them in acceptable English.
3. Let the students hear the conversation again to elicit more of it.

Conversations

1. PRACTICE. *(PAGE 50)*

Competency

[a] Identify common injuries.

Grammar

imperatives (review)

Step-by-Step

1. Play the tape or read the conversation aloud while students follow along in their books.
2. Elicit or demonstrate the meaning of *What happened?, Ahmed fell and cut his head, I think he broke his arm, He needs an ambulance,* and *I'm going to call 911.* Play the tape as many times as students need.
3. Have students repeat the conversation chorally sentence by sentence, and then practice in pairs.

2. WHAT CAN YOU SAY?

Vocabulary

knee, wrist, finger, ankle, cut, break, burn, sprain

Step-by-Step

1. Ask students to look at the pictures and say any words they know. Use the board or OHP and write each word as it is volunteered in a place corresponding to its location on the page. Pronounce each word after you write it and have students point to the word in their books and repeat. Then add any words students have not volunteered. Elicit the base and past form of the verbs.
2. Ask a volunteer to stand and hold up the book for the class to see. (In large classes, make smaller groups with a book held up in each group.) Call on a volunteer to say a sentence and another to point to the picture for the class.
3. Have students work in pairs, one saying a sentence and the other pointing. Then have students write each word several times, and dictate the words to each other in pairs.

Option

Elicit from students other body parts *(head, eye, ear, nose,* and so on) and write them on the board. Have students write the words.

Cross-Reference

The New Oxford Picture Dictionary: The Human Body, pages 4 and 5; and Ailments and Injuries, page 40

3. TALK ABOUT THE INJURIES.

Competency

[a] Identify common injuries.

Step-by-Step

1. Write the conversation on the board or OHP without filling in the handwritten parts. Show students that the information for the blanks comes from the pictures. Fill in the blanks.
2. Read the conversation aloud and have students repeat. Elicit other possible answers from volunteers using *I think she....*
3. Repeat Steps 1 and 2 with the other pictures. Then have pairs of students say the conversation for the class with all the injuries.
4. Have students practice the conversation in pairs, changing partners, saying both parts, and using all the injuries.

Option

Using other parts of the body identified in Option, Exercise 2, have students talk about injuries to other parts of the body. Have them follow the pattern *I think she* _____ *her* _______.

Conversations

4. PRACTICE. *(PAGE 51)*

Grammar

future tense with *be + going to*

Step-by-Step

1. Give students time to look at the picture. Encourage them to guess what Joe, Betty, and Ahmed are saying.
2. Have students close their books. Play the tape or read the conversation. Use the pictures on page 47 of the Teacher's Book or stick figures to indicate which character is speaking each sentence.

3. Have students say anything they can recall of the conversation. Acknowledge all contributions by restating them in acceptable English.
4. Play the tape while students follow along in their books. Then elicit or demonstrate the meaning of *paramedics, emergency room, Don't worry,* and *You're going to be fine.* Stress that *in fifteen minutes* indicates future time. Play the tape as many times as students need.
5. Have students repeat the conversation chorally sentence by sentence and then practice in pairs.

Cross-Reference

The New Oxford Picture Dictionary: Medical and Dental Care, page 39; and Firefighting and Rescue, page 42.

5. FOCUS ON GRAMMAR.

Grammar

future tense with *be + going to*: affirmative and negative statements, *yes/no* questions, *wh-* questions
next week, tomorrow, in fifteen minutes

Step-by-Step

next week, tomorrow, in fifteen minutes

1. Have a volunteer read *I'm going to see the doctor in fifteen minutes.* Write it on the board or OHP in the first column. Read it aloud and have students repeat.
2. Elicit *We are going to see the doctor.* Add *tomorrow.* Write it in the first column, read it, and have students repeat. Repeat Steps 1 and 2, eliciting sentences with *you, they, he,* and *she.* Elicit and write other future time phrases *(next week, next Friday,* or *this afternoon).*

future tense with *be + going to*

3. Draw a circle around *am/is/are going to* and a double line under the base form of the verb. Elicit or show students that *be going to* + the base form of the verb operates as a unit and signals future time. Have volunteers come to the board, circle *be going to,* and draw double lines under the base forms in the examples.

future tense with *be + going to:* affirmative and negative statements and *yes/no* questions

4. In the next column, write *Am I going to see the doctor in fifteen minutes?* Elicit the next question *Are we going to see the doctor tomorrow?,* write it, and have students repeat.
5. In the last column write *I'm not going to see the doctor in fifteen minutes.* Elicit *We aren't going to see the doctor tomorrow,* write it, and have students repeat.
6. Continue this procedure, eliciting negative questions and statements. Write them on the board and have students repeat. Have students copy them.

future tense with *be + going to:* *wh-* questions

7. Have one volunteer read *What are they going to do?* and another read *They are going to see the doctor.* Write the sentences side by side on the board or OHP and have students repeat.
8. Repeat Step 7 with *Where are they going to go?* and *When are they going to go?* Then elicit more *what, where,* and *when* questions and short and long answers with different verbs. Write them on the board, have students repeat, and write them.

Going Further

Contrast the present continuous tense with *be + going to* by writing *now* in one column and *tomorrow* in the other. Elicit *What is he doing now?* and write it under *now.* Elicit *What is he going to do tomorrow?* and write it under *tomorrow.* Continue with different verbs. Have students practice asking and answering questions in both tenses.

6. TALK ABOUT THE PEOPLE.

Grammar

future tense with *be + going to:* affirmative and negative statements, *yes/no* questions, and *wh-* questions

Step-by-Step

1. Write the conversation on the board or OHP without filling in the handwritten parts. Show students that the information for the blanks comes from the cues. Fill in the blanks.
2. Read the conversation aloud and have students repeat. Also have them repeat the other cues. Have pairs of students say the conversation for the class until all the words have been used.
3. Have students practice in pairs, changing partners, saying both parts, and using all the words.

Option

Expand the conversation using as many action words as possible. Add *in an hour, next week,* and other future time expressions.

Conversations

7. PRACTICE. *(PAGE 52)*

b Ask about medical treatment.

c Identify common health problems and treatment.

d Read the names of common medicines.

g Repeat instructions to check your understanding.

Grammar

imperatives (review)

Step-by-Step

1. Have students look at the picture. Encourage them to guess what Ahmed and Dr. Riley are saying.
2. Have students close their books. Play the tape or read the conversation aloud. Use the picture on page 47 of the Teacher's Book and stick figures to indicate who is speaking each sentence.
3. Have students say anything they can recall of the conversation. Acknowledge all contributions by restating them in acceptable English.
4. Play the tape while students follow along in their books. Then elicit or demonstrate the meaning of *Doctor, what can I do for this pain?, pain medicine, prescription, capsules,* and *every four hours.* Play the tape as many times as students need.
5. Have students repeat the conversation sentence by sentence, and practice in pairs.

NOTE: This situation, which depicts a man being treated by a female doctor, might be a culturally sensitive issue for some students.

Pronunciation

Use Minimal Pairs with *you* and *your.* (See page xi.)

Cue	Response
you	This is for you.
your	Your brother is here.

Use Minimal Pairs with *pain* and *pen.*

Cue	Response
pain	pain medicine
pen	Do you have a pen?

8. WHAT CAN YOU SAY?

Vocabulary

backache, capsules, cough, teaspoon, stomachache, tablespoon, fever, tablets

Step-by-Step

1. Ask students to look at the pictures and say any words they can read or guess. Use the board or OHP and write each word as it is volunteered in a place corresponding to its location on the page. After you write each word, say it, and have students point to it in their books and repeat. Add any words students have not volunteered.
2. Ask a volunteer to stand and hold up the book for the class to see. (In large classes, make smaller groups with a book held up in each.) Call on one volunteer to say a word and another to point to the picture.
3. Have student work in pairs, one saying a word and the other pointing. Then have students write each word several times and dictate the words to each other in pairs.

Option

Bring in empty medicine containers including prescription medicine, cough syrup, antacid, and aspirin, as well as capsules, tablets, a teaspoon, and a tablespoon.

9. TALK ABOUT THE MEDICINE.

Competencies

b Ask about medical treatment.

c Identify common health problems and treatment.

Step-by-Step

1. Write the conversation on the board or OHP without filling in the handwritten parts. Show students that the information for the blanks comes from Exercise 8. Fill in the blanks.

2. Read the conversation aloud and have students repeat. Also have them repeat the words in Exercise 8. Have pairs of students say the conversation for the class until all the words have been used.
3. Have students practice in pairs, changing partners, saying both parts, and using all the words in Exercise 8.

NOTE: Many students follow non-Western healing practices, such as *cupping* or *coining*. Others may take herbal medicine or use a shaman. A recognition of varied medical practices could be helpful here. Also stress the importance of following directions when using prescriptions and over-the-counter medications.

Cross-Reference

Multilevel Activity and Resource Package: Grammar

Paperwork

1. READ THE LABELS ON THE MEDICINE IN RAY'S MEDICINE CABINET *(PAGE 53)*

Competency

[d] Read the names of common medicines.

Step-by-Step

1. Draw an outline of the medicine cabinet on the board or OHP. Have students look at the picture and say any words or phrases they can.
2. As each word or phrase is suggested, draw the container, and fill in the name and label on the board. Say the item and have students repeat.
3. Add any word or phrase that students have not volunteered, say it, and have students repeat. Point to items at random and have students read them aloud.
4. Ask questions to confirm students' understanding. *(When do you take cough syrup?* or *How often do you take cold medicine?)*
5. Have students work in pairs, asking and answering questions.

2. MATCH.

Competency

[e] Read and folow instructions on medical labels.

Step-by-Step

1. Copy the exercise on the board or OHP.
2. Have students identify the pictures in the first column, say the words, and have students repeat.
3. Read the first item in the second column. *(Take two teaspoons at bedtime.)* Elicit which picture matches these directions and draw a line between the two. Have students match *bedtime* with *10:30 p.m.* in the last column. Have a volunteer draw a line between the two items.
4. Pair students and have them match the items in their books. Have volunteers match items on the board. Have other volunteers read the matched sets.

Cross-Reference

Multilevel Activity and Resource Package: Concentration 1

Going Further

Use imperatives to give instructions for taking medicine. Have students mime the instructions with actual teaspoons, tablespoons, capsules, and so on.

Check understanding by drawing several clock faces on the board. Have students draw in the hands to indicate when to take the dosages.

3. INTERVIEW THREE CLASSMATES.

Gives practice in speaking and writing.

Step-by-Step

1. Copy the questions on the board or OHP without filling in Ray's information.
2. Invite a student to speak for Ray. Interview "Ray" and fill in the examples on the board.
3. Read the interview questions and have students repeat.
4. Invite a student to interview you and write your answers on the grid. Correct any errors with the whole class.
5. Have students ask and answer the questions with three classmates and write their answers on a separate piece of paper.

Cross-Reference

Multilevel Activity and Resource Package: Scrambled Sentences and Listening

Reading and Writing

1. WHAT CAN YOU SAY ABOUT AHMED? WHAT CAN YOU SAY ABOUT THE DOCTOR? *(PAGE 54)*

Pre-reading.

Step-by-Step

1. Have students look at the pictures and say anything they can about Ahmed. As each word, phrase, or sentence is suggested, write it on the board or OHP, say it, and have students repeat.
2. Add any key words, phrases, or sentences that have not been volunteered. Point to items at random and have students read them aloud.
3. Repeat for Dr. Riley.

2. READ ABOUT AHMED.

Reading.

Step-by-Step

1. Give students time to look at the story and read what they can. Then play the tape or read the story aloud while students follow in their books.
2. Play the tape one sentence at a time and have students repeat. Then have volunteers read sentences aloud.

3. CIRCLE YES, NO, OR I DON'T KNOW.

Comprehension check.

Step-by-Step

1. Write *Did Ahmed break his arm?* and *Yes, No, I don't know* side by side on the board or OHP. Elicit the answer and circle it.
2. Have volunteers read the remaining questions and write them on the board.
3. Pair students to complete the exercise in their books. Have volunteers circle their answers on the board. Then correct the answers with the whole class.

Going Further

For items with *I don't know* answers, ask students to elaborate with by making a guess with *I think*______.

Cross-Reference

Multilevel Activity and Resource Package: Picture Story

Reading and Writing

4. SUMI GOT SICK... *(PAGE 55)*

Pre-reading.

Step-by-Step

1. Have students look at the pictures and say anything they can. As each word, phrase, or sentence is suggested, write it on the board or OHP, say it, and have students repeat.
2. Add any key words from the reading in Exercise 5 that students have not volunteered. Point to items at random and have students read them aloud.
3. Read *Sumi got sick and went to the doctor. The doctor gave Sumi instructions. What is Sumi going to do?* Elicit responses with *be + going to.*

5. READ ABOUT SUMI.

Reading.

Step-by-Step

1. Give students time to look at the story and read what they can. Then play the tape or read the story aloud while students follow in their books.
2. Elicit the meaning of *flu, sore throat, liquids,* and *a few days.* Play the tape one sentence at a time and have students repeat. Then have volunteers read sentences of the story aloud.

Going Further

Reinforce your school's policy on absences. Have students make mock phone calls to inform the school and give a reason.

6. YOU ARE SUMI'S DOCTOR...

Comprehension check and writing.

Step-by-Step

1. Write *Stay in bed and rest* on the board or OHP. Show students that the other instructions come from Exercise 4. Read the instructions in Exercise 4 and have students repeat.
2. Elicit *Take two aspirin every four hours,* write it, read it, and have students repeat.
3. Leave the instructions on the board as a model. Have pairs of students complete the exercise in their books. Send one partner to the board to write their sentences. Then correct the answers with the whole class, and call on the other partner to read their sentences from the board.

NOTE: Students may ask about *two aspirin. Aspirin* is both singular and plural.

Pronunciation

Use The Human Computer™ with the instructions on the board. (See page xii.)

7. A, YOU ARE SUMI'S DOCTOR...

Competency

[f] Follow simple instructions for medical treatment.

Step-by-Step

1. Write *Stay in bed and rest* on the board or OHP. Have a volunteer read the doctor's instructions aloud. Take Sumi's part and act out lying in bed and resting.

2. Elicit other instructions, using the words in Exercise 4. Have different pairs of students say and follow the instructions using actual items or pictures of them which you have brought in.
3. Have students practice in pairs, using all the cues, and saying both parts.

Cross-Reference

Multilevel Activity and Resource Package: Writing, Sorting, Jigsaw Reading, and Sequencing

Option

Practice clarification strategies with medical instructions by having students repeat the doctor's instructions with a rising intonation. Have the doctor say *That's right,* or repeat the instructions.

Listening Plus

1. WHAT'S NEXT? *(PAGE 56)*

Predicting with social and grammatical clues.

Step-by-Step

1. With students' books closed, write the first response in *a* on the board or OHP. Read it aloud and have students repeat.
2. Have students work in pairs to imagine what might come before.
3. Have pairs volunteer their ideas. Help the class evaluate each one.
4. Do the same with the other responses in *a* and leave the responses on the board.
5. Have students open their books and a volunteer come to the board.
6. Play the tape or read the tapescript aloud one conversation at a time. Have students point to the correct response in their books and have the volunteer point to it at the board. Play the tape as many times as students need.
7. Repeat the process for *b.*

2. REVIEW...WRITE...NUMBER.

Focused listening

ANSWER KEY

Write: a. *aspirin;* b. *pain medicine;* c. *stitches;* d. *antacid;* e. *bandage;* f. *X-ray*

Number: a. *3;* b. *6;* c. *5;* d. *2;* e. *4;* f. *1*

REVIEW.

Step-by-Step

1. Have students look at the picture and read or say anything they can about the people.
2. Have students brainstorm all the names of medical treatments that have been introduced in the unit, especially those they will need to write *(stitches, pain medicine, X-rays, aspirin, bandage,* and *antacid).* As names of the treatments are volunteered, write them on the board or OHP, say them, and have students repeat.
3. Point to items on the board at random and have volunteers read them aloud.

WRITE.

Step-by-Step

1. Copy the answer blanks on the board or OHP.
2. Play the tape or read the first conversation aloud. Fill in the first answer as students hear it.
3. Continue playing one conversation at a time and have students fill in the other answers. Play the tape as many times as students need.
4. Have students compare their answers in pairs.
5. Play the tape again, one conversation at a time. Have a volunteer write the answers on the board. Correct the student's answers with the whole class.
6. Have students check their answers against the answers on the board, then play the tape once more so that students can verify their answers.

NUMBER.

Step-by-Step

1. Play the tape or read the tapescript aloud one conversation at a time, as many times as students need. Have students number the pictures in the order of the conversations they hear.
2. Have students compare their answers in pairs.
3. Play the tape again and have a volunteer write the answers on the board. Correct any errors with the whole class.
4. Have students check their answers against the answers on the board, then play the tape once more so that students can verify their answers.

3. A, TELL ABOUT A PATIENT IN 2.

Speaking and active listening.

Step-by-Step

1. Have volunteers make statements about one of the patients in Exercise 2. Repeat each statement. Demonstrate the use of clarification strategies (for example, repetition to confirm understanding—*He burned his foot?)*.
2. Have students hold up their books and point to the person described.
3. Have students work in pairs to make statements, restate, and point. Each student should change partners and describe all the people. Circulate to listen and give help as needed.

4. WHAT ABOUT YOU?

Listening and responding with personal information.

Step-by-Step

1. Play the tape once. Have students confer in groups to reconstruct the statement they heard. Circulate to hear what they say.
2. Repeat Step 1 until most groups have the gist of the statement.
3. Have groups share their reconstructions and help them reach a consensus.
4. Play the tape again so that students can verify their reconstruction.
5. Have students answer the question on the tape by writing similar information about themselves. Encourage students to vary or extend their answers. Circulate to give help and feedback.
6. Have several volunteers put their answers on the board. Help the volunteers extend their answers if they have not already done so. Correct any errors with the whole class.
7. Have students compare their own answers with the answers on the board, then check each other's answers in pairs.

Cross-Reference

Multilevel Activity and Resource Package: Go Fish and Concentration 2

Interactions

1. & 2. GET INFORMATION/GIVE INFORMATION. *(PAGES 57 AND 58)*

Competency

g Repeat instructions to check your understanding.

Vocabulary

common health problems, body parts, medical treatment

Step-by-Step

1. Write the conversation on the board or OHP without filling in the handwritten parts. Review the vocabulary related to the symptoms and treatment of coughs, fevers, sprained ankles, stomachaches, colds, and backaches.

2. Hold up your book and show students the two pages. Divide the class into a Student A group and a Student B group, and have them open their books to their group's page. Show them where Student A gets her questions and where B gets the answers.
3. Read the conversation aloud and have students repeat. Have a volunteer from each group say the conversation for the class.
4. Erase the information in the blanks. Call on other volunteers to say the conversation using the next cue. Fill in the blanks.
5. Have A's and B's work in pairs to fill in the information. Each student should change partners and do both parts.

Cross-Reference

Multilevel Activity and Resource Package: Categories and Game: "C" Search

Progress Checks

1. MATCH. *(PAGE 59)*

Competencies

c Identify common health problems and treatment.

d Read the names of common medicines.

Have students match the health problem with the treatment.

2. MATCH.

Competency

e Read and follow instructions on medicine labels.

Have students match the dosages and medicine labels, as they did on page 53, Exercise 2.

Progress Checks

3. WHAT HAPPENED? TELL YOUR PARTNER. *(PAGE 60)*

Competency

a Identify common injuries.

Have pairs of students work together asking *What happened?* and answering with descriptions of the situation, who the people might be, and what they are saying.

Basic Statements

She broke her wrist.
He burned his finger.
He sprained his ankle.
She cut her toe.

4. WHAT ARE THE PEOPLE SAYING?/ DO IT YOURSELF.

Competencies

b Ask about medical treatment.

g Repeat instructions to check your understanding.

f Follow simple instructions for medical treatment.

Basic Conversation

A: *Stay in bed and rest./Stay home and rest.*
B: *Stay in bed and rest?/Stay home and rest?*
A: *Yes.*

Option

In *Do It Yourself,* students should not limit themselves to the example instruction in *What Are the People Saying?* Students should add more doctor's instructions which the patient acts out to demonstrate competency.

Memo to the Teacher

Option

Take students to a drug store or pharmacy section of a supermarket. Have students look for different types of common products for specific ailments. Have students work in pairs to choose one product for each health problem, read the label, and fill in a chart:

Injury or Health Problem	Product	Dosage
1. stomachache	______	______
2. cut finger	______	______
3. sore throat	______	______

BEFORE CLASS

Back in the classroom, have students compile a master list on the board, including all the products they found for each problem.

UNIT 6 Food

COMPETENCIES	GRAMMAR
Offer to help someone • Respond to offers of help • Ask for clarification using basic question words • Read prices, weights, measures for food, and abbreviations • State likes and dislikes	count and noncount nouns *some, any, much, many, a lot of* questions with *how many/ how much* + count/noncount nouns

Warm-ups

BEFORE  CLASS

1. Do It or Draw It! (Use at any point in the unit.) Write specific commands on slips of paper *(eat a banana, cook a hamburger, wash the dishes,* and so on). Divide the class into two teams. Have a person from one team select a paper, and then act out the command or draw it. The team has two minutes to guess the command. If the team guesses before the time limit, they score one point. When the time is up, the second team takes a turn with a new command.

2. I'm Going to the Supermarket (Use after page 62.)
Divide students into two or more teams. Teams are to think of a food item for each letter of the alphabet *(A–apple, B–banana,* etc.). Set a time limit. The team with the most right answers wins.

BEFORE  CLASS

3. Stand Up Bingo (Use after page 67.)
Hand out Food Word Cards from the *Multilevel Activity and Resource Package,* or make your own cards. Arrange chairs with the same number of students sitting across and down the rows, like the squares on a Bingo card. Call out words students have at random. Students with the picture of that food item stand. Continue until a row of students is standing in a horizontal, vertical, or diagonal line.

Getting Started

1. GUESS. *(PAGE 61)*

Establishes the context of the unit.

Step-by-Step

1. Have students look at the pictures and point out Ramona and Mrs. Wilson.
2. Give students time to look at the picture on page 58 of the Teacher's Book. Have them identify Ramona as a student from Mexico. Mrs. Wilson is her neighbor. Then ask where the characters are. Have students identify as many items in the picture they can.
3. Ask students to guess what Ramona and Mrs. Wilson are saying. All responses are valid here. Respond to each guess by restating it in acceptable English.

2. WHAT CAN YOU HEAR?

Prepares students to read the first conversation on page 62.

Step-by-Step

1. Have students look at the picture while you play the tape or read the conversation aloud.
2. Have students volunteer any words or sentences they can recall from the conversation. Acknowledge all contributions by restating them in acceptable English.
3. Let the students hear the conversation again to elicit more of it.

Conversations

1. PRACTICE. *(PAGE 62)*

Grammar

count/noncount nouns
some, any

Step-by-Step

1. Play the tape or read the conversation aloud while students follow along in their books.
2. Elicit or demonstrate the meaning of *Come in, supermarket, Do you need anything?, You're very kind, Now let me see, some tea, some bread, any potatoes,* and *some onions.*
3. Have students repeat the conversation chorally sentence by sentence and then practice in pairs.

2. WHAT CAN YOU SAY?

Vocabulary

tea, bread, ice cream, potatoes, onions, apples

Step-by-Step

1. Ask students to look at the pictures and say any words they can. Use the board or OHP and write each word as it is volunteered in a place corresponding to its location on the page. After you write each word, say it, and have students point to it in their books and repeat. Add any words students have not volunteered. Elicit the observation that the items in the top row do not end in *-s*, while those in the bottom row do. Count the items in the bottom row *(one potato, two potatoes,* and so on).
2. Ask a volunteer to stand and hold up the book for the class to see. (In large classes, make smaller groups with a book held up in each.) Call on one volunteer to say a word and another to point to the picture.
3. Have students work in pairs, one saying a word and the other pointing. Then have students write each word several times, and dictate the words to each other in pairs.

NOTE: Some languages do not make a distinction between count/noncount nouns, so this will present a teaching challenge. For other languages, the concept will be familiar, but specific items will have to be reassigned into new count or noncount categories.

3. FOCUS ON GRAMMAR.

Grammar

count/noncount nouns
some, any

Step-by-Step

1. Have one volunteer read *Do you need any tea?* and another read *Yes, I need some tea.* Write both sentences on the board or OHP side by side, read them, and have students repeat.
2. Write *bread* in the left column and elicit *Do you need any bread?* and its corresponding answer *Yes, I need some bread.* Write both sentences on the board, read them, and have students repeat.
3. Continue with other nouns *(ice cream, potatoes, onions,* and *apples)*. Elicit the rule that *any* is used in questions and *some* is used in affirmative statements.
4. Have a volunteer read *No, I don't need any tea.* Write it in a third column, read it and have students repeat. Elicit the rule that *any* is used with negative statements.
5. Elicit other negative statements, write them, read them, and have students repeat. Elicit the observation that *some* and *any* are used with *tea, potatoes, bread, onions, ice cream,* and *apples* in various statement and question forms, and that *some* is used with the plural form of *potatoes, onions,* and *apples.*
6. Have students copy the sentences on a separate piece of paper.

4. TALK ABOUT YOURSELF.

Competencies

a Offer to help someone.

b Respond to offers of help.

Grammar

some, any

Step-by-Step

1. Write the conversation on the board or OHP without filling in the handwritten parts. Show students that the information for the blanks comes from Exercise 2.
2. Fill in the blanks. Read the conversation sentence by sentence and have students repeat. Then read the food list in Exercise 2.
3. Have a volunteer say the conversation with you. Then have volunteers say the conversation with all the other words.
4. Have students practice in pairs, changing partners, saying both parts, and using all the food.

Option

Have students use other food items they know.

Conversations

5. PRACTICE. *(PAGE 63)*

Grammar

much, many, a lot of

Step-by-Step

1. Give students time to look at the picture of Ramona and Mrs. Wilson (page 61), who are still talking. Encourage them to guess what they are saying.
2. Have students close their books. Play the tape or read the conversation. Use Ramona's picture and draw a stick figure of Mrs. Wilson to indicate who is speaking each line.
3. Have students say anything they can recall of the conversation. Acknowledge all contributions by restating them in acceptable English.
4. Play the tape while students follow along in their books. Then elicit or demonstrate the meaning of *really, cookies, How about?, cake, much, rice, a lot of, bananas,* and *many.* Play the tape as many times as students need.
5. Have students repeat the conversation sentence by sentence, and practice in pairs.

6. FOCUS ON GRAMMAR.

Grammar

much, many, a lot of

Step-by-Step

much, a lot of

1. Have one volunteer read *Do you eat much rice?,* another read *Yes, I eat a lot of rice,* and a third read *No, I don't eat much rice.* Write the sentences in three columns on the board. Read the sentences aloud and have students repeat.
2. Provide another noun *(cake)*, have students complete the question and affirmative and negative answers, and write them in the appropriate columns. Read the sentences aloud and have students repeat.

   Elicit the observation that *much* is used in questions and negative statements and that *a lot of* is used in affirmative sentences.

   Draw a single line under *much rice* and *much cake* in the examples.

many, a lot of

3. Continue the chart by writing *many bananas* in the first column and underlining it twice. Elicit *a lot of bananas* for the second column, and *many bananas* for the third. Write the sentences on the board, read them, and have students repeat.

   Elicit the observation that *much* is used with *rice, cake, tea, bread,* and *ice cream,* and *many* is used with *potatoes, onions, apples, cookies,* and *bananas* in questions and negative statements. *A lot of* is used with all nouns in affirmative statements.
4. Have students copy the sentences. Pair students and have them generate sentences using new food items, verbs, and pronouns.
5. Have volunteers write their sentences on the board, correct any errors with the whole class, and call on volunteers to read the sentences on the board.

Going Further

Say a food word and cue students by saying *question, yes,* or *no.* Have students say a sentence which follows the grammar chart on the board.

T: *Bread. Question.*
S: *Do you eat much bread?*
T: *No.*
S: *No, I don't eat much bread.*
T: *Apples.*
S: *No, I don't eat many apples.*

7. TALK ABOUT THE BOY.

Grammar

count and noncount nouns
much, many, a lot of

Step-by-Step

1. Write the conversation on the board or OHP without filling in the handwritten parts. Show students that the information for the blanks comes from the lists. Fill in the blanks.
2. Read the conversation aloud and have students repeat. Have them repeat the words in the list. Elicit that *many* is used with *apples, potatoes, cookies,* and *bananas* in questions and negative statements. Give students a cue *(bread)* and have them say *much* or *many (much bread)*.
3. Have pairs of students say the conversation for the class until all the words have been used.
4. Have students practice in pairs, changing partners, saying both parts, and using all the words.

Cross-Reference

Multilevel Activity and Resource Package:
Concentration 1

Conversations

8. WHAT CAN YOU SAY? *(PAGE 64)*

Vocabulary

a box, a bottle, a loaf, a jar, a bag, a can

Step-by-Step

1. Ask students to look at the pictures and say any words they can. Write each word as it is volunteered on the board or OHP in a place corresponding to its location on the page. After you write each word, say it, and have students point to it in their books and repeat. Add any words students have not volunteered.
2. Ask a volunteer to stand and hold up the book for the class to see. (In large classes, make smaller groups with a book held up in each.) Call one one volunteer to say a word and another to point to the picture.
3. Have students work in pairs, one saying a word and the other pointing. Then have students write each word several times and dictate the words to each other in pairs.

Cross-Reference

The New Oxford Picture Dictionary: Containers, Quantities, and Money, pages 12 and 13

9. PRACTICE.

Grammar

questions with *how many/how much* + count/ noncount nouns

Step-by-Step

1. Have students close their books and listen to the continuation of Ramona and Mrs. Wilson's conversation. Play the tape or read the conversation aloud. Use the picture of Ramona and a stick figure of Mrs. Wilson to indicate which character is speaking each sentence.
2. Have students say anything they can recall of the conversation. Acknowledge all contributions by restating them in acceptable English.
3. Play the tape while students follow along in their books. Then elicit or demonstrate the meaning of *How many onions?* and *How much bread?* Play the tape as many times as students need.
4. Have students repeat the conversation sentence by sentence, and practice in pairs.

Pronunciation

Use Imitation and Correction with plurals: *boxes, bottles, loaves, jars, bags, cans,* and *onions.* (See page xi.)

10. FOCUS ON GRAMMAR.

Grammar

questions with *how many/how much* + count/ noncount nouns

Step-by-Step

questions with *how much* + noncount nouns

1. Have one volunteer read *How much bread do you want?*, another read *A small loaf,* and a third read *Two small loaves.* Write the sentences in three columns. Elicit that the plural of *loaf* is *loaves.* Read the three items and have students repeat.
2. Write *tea* in the first column and elicit the complete question and the two answers. If necessary, have students refer to the list of containers in Exercise 8. Elicit that *how much* is used with *bread, tea, oil, peanut butter,* and *rice.* Then elicit the containers *(cans, jars, bags,* and so on) which indicate a specific amount.
3. Elicit more examples for all three columns, write them, read them, and have students repeat.

questions with *how many* + count nouns

4. Repeat Steps 1, 2, and 3 with *How many onions do you want?* and then *How many potatoes?* If necessary, refer to the food pictures in Exercise 2, page 62 and Exercise 7, page 63. Elicit that the plural form *onions, potatoes, apples, cookies,* and *bananas* is used with *how many,* and that the response can be either singular or plural.
5. Have students copy the items. Then have students work in pairs to generate other sentences both orally and in writing. Send volunteers to the board to write their sentences, correct any errors with the whole class, and call on volunteers to read sentences from the board.

11. TALK ABOUT THE FOOD.

Competency

c Ask for clarification using basic question words.

Grammar

questions with *how many/how much* + count/ noncount nouns

Vocabulary

teabags, peanut butter, oil

Step-by-Step

1. Write the conversation on the board or OHP without filling in the handwritten parts. Show students that the information for the blanks comes from the pictures and captions. Fill in the blanks.
2. Read the conversation aloud and have students repeat. Also repeat the names for all the food items, containers, and sizes. Have students repeat. Read the cues again and have volunteers say *how much* or *how many (Peanut butter. How much?/ Potatoes. How many?).*
3. Have pairs of students say the conversation for the class until all the words have been used. Have students practice in pairs, changing partners, saying both parts, and using all the words.

Cross-Reference

Multilevel Activity and Resource Package: Word Tap and Listening

Paperwork

1. READ THE ADVERTISEMENT. *(PAGE 65)*

Competency

d Read prices, weights, measures for food, and abbreviations.

Vocabulary

food weights, measures, and abbreviations

Step-by-Step

1. Draw an outline of the advertisement on the board or OHP. Have students look at the ad in their books and read aloud any words or phrases they can. As each word is said, write it in the appropriate place, say it aloud, and have students repeat. Have students read the slash (/) as *a*. *(Gloreo cookies are 75 cents a package.)*
2. Elicit or supply missing items in the same way. If necessary, clarify the meaning of the weights, measures, and food abbreviations. Show that most abbreviations are created by dropping out some letters *(package = pkg.)*, but there are exceptions *(pound = lb.,* or *ounce = oz.).*
3. Ask questions to check and confirm students' understanding. *(How much are Gloreo cookies? What costs 55 cents a pound? What does gal. mean?)* Point to items in the completed ad at random and have students read them aloud.

Going Further

Bring in food ads to compare local prices with those in the book. Have students group items that are measured by volume or by weight.

Bring in empty cup, quart, and gallon containers. Have students measure to determine the number of cups in a quart, the number of quarts in a gallon, and so on.

2. WRITE THE ABBREVIATIONS.

Writing food abbreviations.

Step-by-Step

1. Write the measurements on the board or OHP.
2. Have students refer to the abbreviations in Exercise 1, page 65. Ask volunteers to spell the appropriate abbreviation. Write it on the board.
3. Erase the abbreviations. Have students complete the exercise in their books. Have volunteers write their answers on the board and have students check their work.

Going Further

Have students write as many words for weights and measures as they can *(a pound, a dozen,* and so on) in columns on a separate piece of paper. Have students in small groups list the food they buy under the correct weight or measure category *(a dozen/doughnuts, eggs; a pound/meat, apples)*. Have groups write their lists on the board. The group with the longest list wins.

Pronunciation

Use Imitation and Correction with *apples, bananas,* and *gallon.* (See page xi.) Listen for the vowel sound in the stressed syllables, which is made by placing the tongue far forward in the bottom of the mouth. Have students think of other words with the same stressed vowel.

3. INTERVIEW THREE CLASSMATES.

Competency

e State likes and dislikes.

Step-by-Step

1. Copy the interview questions and answers on the board or OHP. Tell students that these are Ramona's answers and have students repeat.
2. Interview a volunteer and fill in his answers with students' help.
3. Have a volunteer interview you and write your answers on the board. Encourage the student to use clarification strategies if he needs to. Correct the answers on the board with the whole class.
4. Have each student ask three classmates the questions and write their answers on a separate piece of paper.

Cross-Reference

Multilevel Activity and Resource Package: Concentration 2

Going Further

Have students share their completed interviews with two other students. Have them use complete sentences. *(José shops at Kings Club. He likes milk. He doesn't like apple juice.)*

Reading and Writing

1. DONNA WANTS TO MAKE A TACO SALAD. WHAT CAN YOU SAY ABOUT THE FOOD SHE NEEDS? *(PAGE 66)*

Pre-reading.

Step-by-Step

1. Have students look at the picture and say any words or sentences they can about it. Encourage students to use complete sentences. *(Donna needs a pound of beef. She is going to buy a pound of beef.)* As each word or sentence is suggested, write it, say it, and have students repeat.
2. Add any phrases or sentences that students have not volunteered. Use the pictures to teach new words *(a head of lettuce, cheese, tomatoes,* and *corn chips)*. Point to items at random and have students read them aloud.

2. READ ABOUT DONNA.

Reading stories.

Step-by-Step

1. Give students time to look at the story and read what they can. Then play the tape or read the story aloud while students follow in their books.
2. Play the tape one sentence at a time and have students repeat. Then have volunteers read sentences from the story aloud.

Going Further

Have students rewrite the story changing the pronouns and tenses. Begin: *Yesterday I wanted to make a taco salad for dinner,* or *Every week we make a taco salad for dinner.* Have students make the necessary changses throughout.

Pronunciation

Use Minimal Pairs with *she's* and *cheese.* (See page xi.) The initial consonants in these two words are identical except that *cheese* begins with a momentary complete stoppage of the flow of air.

Cue	Response
she's	She's at the store.
cheese	a pound of cheese

3. FILL IN THE BLANKS WITH THE AMOUNTS. USE ABBREVIATIONS.

Comprehension check.

Step-by-Step

1. Draw an outline of the shopping list on the board or OHP. Write *ground beef* first. Ask *How much ground beef is Donna going to buy?* Have a volunteer spell the answer and write *1 lb.* in the first blank.
2. Pair students to complete the exercise in their books. Have volunteers read the complete list as you write it on the board. Have volunteers write their answers on the board. Then correct the answers with the whole class.

Cross-Reference

Multilevel Activity and Resource Package: Go Fish, Picture Story, and Jigsaw Reading

Going Further

Have students work in pairs asking and answering questions about Donna's list. *(How much cheese is she going to buy?)*

Reading and Writing

4. LOOK AT THE FOODS. ADD OTHER FOODS YOU KNOW. CIRCLE THE FOODS YOU LIKE. *(PAGE 67)*

Pre-writing.

Step-by-Step

1. Write the words on the board or OHP in columns in the correct order. Read each item aloud and have students repeat. Write additional items on the board as students volunteer them. Leave the list on the board as a model.
2. Have students complete the list in their books. Help with spelling as needed.
3. Say *I like eggs* and circle *eggs* on the board. Have students circle foods they like in their books. Circulate and answer questions as needed.

Going Further

Have students review their lists and classify items into groups of foods sold by the pound, in packages, in cans, and so on. Tell students that some items may be in more than one group.

5. WRITE A SHOPPING LIST FOR DINNER. USE THE LIST IN 3 AS AN EXAMPLE. EXPLAIN YOUR SHOPPING LIST TO YOUR PARTNER.

Writing.

Step-by-Step

1. Have students choose dishes for a dinner they would like to prepare for three friends. Write several of their suggestions on the board.
2. Have students list the ingredients for each dish on the board and estimate quantities.
3. Have students complete their own lists using Donna's as a model.
4. Have students show their lists to their partner, tell what they are going to make, and show the ingredients for each dish.

6. ANSWER THESE QUESTIONS ABOUT YOUR SHOPPING LIST. USE *SOME* AND *ANY.*

Comprehension check.

Step-by-Step

1. Write your own shopping list on the board or OHP. Then write *Are you going to buy any apples?* on the board, read it, and then refer to your own shopping list. Answer the question with either *Yes, I'm going to buy some apples* or *No, I'm not going to buy any apples.* Write your answer on the line.
2. Have students in pairs write their answers in their books. Circulate and help with any questions.
3. Write the remaining questions on the board. Have volunteers write their answers in two columns, one for affirmative statements with *some,* the other for negative statements with *any.* Then check the answers with the whole class.

Option

Have students write their partner's answers on a separate piece of paper using *He* or *She.*

Cross-Reference

Multilevel Activity and Resource Package: Grammar, Categories, and Writing

Listening Plus

1. WHAT'S NEXT? *(PAGE 68)*

Predicting with social and grammatical clues.

Step-by-Step

1. Have students close their books. Write the first response in *a* on the board or OHP. Read it aloud and have students repeat.
2. Have students work in pairs to imagine what might come before.
3. Have pairs volunteer their ideas. Help the class evaluate each one.
4. Do the same with the other responses in *a* and leave the responses on the board.
5. Have students open their books and a volunteer come to the board.

6. Play the tape or read the tapescript aloud one conversation at a time. Have students point to the correct response in their books and have the volunteer point to it at the board. Play the tape as many times as students need.
7. Repeat the process for *b*.

2. REVIEW...WRITE...NUMBER.

Focused listening.

ANSWER KEY

Write: a. *89¢;* b. *$4.99;* c. *99¢;* d. *$2.99;* e. *$2.19;* f. *$2.29;* g. *$1.29;* h. *89¢;* i. *$1.89*

Number: a. *4 ;* b. *3;* c. *5;* d. *7;* e. *1 ;* f. *9;* g. *6;* h. *8;* i. *2*

REVIEW.

Step-by-Step

1. Have students look at the pictures and read or say anything they can about the items.
2. As vocabulary from the unit is volunteered, write it on the board or OHP, say it, and have students repeat.
3. Elicit any other vocabulary which will be helpful in distinguishing among the items.
4. Point to items on the board at random and have volunteers read them aloud.

WRITE.

Step-by-Step

1. Copy the answer blanks on the board or OHP.
2. Play the tape or read the first conversation aloud. Fill in the first answer as students hear it.
3. Continue playing one conversation at a time and have students fill in the other answers. Play the tape as many times as students need.
4. Have students compare their answers in pairs.
5. Play the tape again, one conversation at a time. Have a volunteer write the answers on the board. Correct the student's answers with the whole class.
6. Have students check their answers against the answers on the board, then play the tape once more so that students can verify their answers.

NUMBER.

Step-by-Step

1. Play the tape or read the tapescript aloud one conversation at a time, as many times as students need. Have students number the pictures in the order of the conversations they hear.
2. Have students compare their answers in pairs.
3. Play the tape again and have a volunteer write the answers on the board. Correct any errors with the whole class.
4. Have students check their answers against the answers on the board, then play the tape once more so that students can verify their answers.

3. A, TELL ABOUT THE PICTURES IN 2.

Speaking and active listening.

Step-by-Step

1. Have volunteers make statements about one of the items in Exercise 2. Repeat each statement. Demonstrate the use of clarification strategies (for example, *How much?, How many?,* or *What size?).*
2. Have students hold up their books and point to the item described.
3. Have students work in pairs to make statements, restate, and point. Each student should change partners and describe all the items. Circulate to listen and give help as needed.

4. WHAT ABOUT YOU?

Listening and responding with personal information.

Step-by-Step

1. Play the tape once. Have students confer in groups to reconstruct the statement they heard. Circulate to hear what they say.
2. Repeat Step 1 until most groups have the gist of the statement.
3. Have groups share their reconstructions and help them reach a consensus.
4. Play the tape again so that students can verify their reconstruction.

5. Have students answer the question on the tape by writing similar information about themselves. Encourage students to vary or extend their answers. Circulate to give help and feedback.
6. Have several volunteers put their answers on the board. Help the volunteers extend their answers if they have not already done so. Correct any errors with the whole class.
7. Have students compare their own answers with the answers on the board, then check each other's answers in pairs.

Interactions

1. & 2. GET INFORMATION/GIVE INFORMATION. *(PAGES 69 AND 70)*

Grammar

questions with *how many/how much* + count/ noncount nouns

Step-by-Step

1. Write the conversation on the board or OHP without filling in the handwritten parts. Review the food items pictured, their containers, and weight, if necessary.
2. Divide the class into a Student A group and a Student B group, and have them open their books to their group's page. Have the Student A group point to the items on their list and the B group point to the pictured items.
3. Fill in the conversation, read it aloud sentence by sentence, and have students repeat. Have volunteers from both groups say the conversation. Erase the information in the blanks. Call on new volunteers to say the conversation using *bananas.* Fill in the blanks.
4. Have students work in pairs to fill in their lists. Each student should change partners and do both pages.

Cross-Reference

Multilevel Activity and Resource Package: Game: Food Bingo

Progress Checks

1. FILL IN THE AD. USE THESE PRICES. *(PAGE 71)*

Competency

[d] Read prices, weights, measures for food, and abbreviations.

2. WHAT IS SHE SAYING?/ DO IT YOURSELF.

Competency

[e] State likes and dislikes.

Basic Conversation

A: *I don't like oranges. I like apples.*

Have students talk about food items they know.

Progress Checks

3. WHAT ARE THE PEOPLE SAYING?/ DO IT YOURSELF. *(PAGE 72)*

Competencies

[a] Offer to help someone.

[b] Respond to offers of help.

Basic Conversation

A: *We're going to the drugstore. Do you need anything?*
B: *No, thank you.*
A: *We're going to the supermarket, too. Do you need any milk?*
B: *Yes, thanks. I need two quarts of milk.*

Have students write separate shopping lists for the supermarket, the drugstore, etc., and use their lists to answer each other's questions.

4. WHAT ARE THE PEOPLE SAYING?/ DO IT YOURSELF.

Competency

[c] Ask for clarification using basic question words.

Basic Conversation

A: *She wants two quarts of milk.*
B: *How many quarts?*
A: *Two.*

Students can talk to new partners, reporting the requests of their partners in Exercise 3.

Memo to the Teacher

BEFORE

CLASS

Option

Have students go to a supermarket and fill in a form.

Store:
Location:
Date:

Brand	Food	Price	Size
1. Slanter's	peanut butter	$2.89	8 oz.
2.	milk		
3.	rice		
4.	______		

In class, have students compare the information they collected.

UNIT 7 Finding a Job

COMPETENCIES	GRAMMAR
Ask about job openings • Set a time for a job interview • Answer questions about work experience • Fill out a simple job application form • Answer questions about work shifts, hours, and starting dates	*can:* affirmative and negative statements; *yes/no* questions; *yes/no* short answers past tense of *be:* affirmative and negative statements; *yes/no* questions; *yes/no* short answers

Warm-ups

BEFORE

CLASS

1. Interview Introductions (Use at any point in the unit.)
Take the role of an interviewer *(B)* and have a volunteer take the role of a job applicant *(A)*. Model an introduction by shaking hands firmly and saying:

A: *Hello. I'm ______.*
B: *I'm ______. I'm glad to meet you.* (handshake)
A: *I'm glad to meet you, too.*
B: *Please have a seat, Ms./Miss/Mrs./Mr.______.*
A: *Thank you, Ms./Miss/Mrs./Mr.______.*

Have students introduce themselves, changing partners several times.

2. Brainstorm (Use after page 74.)
Write the names of countries represented in your class (including the U.S.) on the board or OHP. Ask students *How do people get a job in your country?* Write their answers (words, phrases, or sentences) on the board under the appropriate country and compare different employment customs.

3. What Do I Do? (Use after page 74.)
Write occupations on self-stick labels. Stick a label on each student's back. Have students circulate, asking each other *yes/no* questions until they can all guess their own occupations.

Getting Started

1. GUESS. *(PAGE 73)*

Establishes the context of the unit.

Step-by-Step

1. Have students look at the pictures of Sue and Ms. Garber and ask where they are.
2. Have students look at the picture on page 69 of the Teacher's Book and identify Sue Lee as a student and guess that Ms. Garber is a secretary.
3. Ask students to guess what they are saying. All responses are valid here. Respond to each guess by restating it in acceptable English.

Going Further

Write *Miss, Mrs., Ms.,* and *Mr.* on the board and elicit the meaning of each abbreviation. Indicate that *Mr.* is the only term used for men and that it does not indicate marital status.

2. WHAT CAN YOU HEAR?

Prepares students to read the first conversation on page 74.

Step-by-Step

1. Have students look at the pictures while you play the tape or read the conversation aloud.
2. Have students volunteer any words or sentences they can recall from the conversation. Acknowledge all contributions by restating them in acceptable English.
3. Let the students hear the conversation again to elicit more of it.

Conversations

1. PRACTICE. *(PAGE 74)*

Vocabulary

May I help you?, openings for sewing machine operators

Step-by-Step

1. Play the tape or read the conversation aloud while students follow along in their books.
2. Elicit or demonstrate the meaning of any key words or phrases by referring to the pictures on pages 73 and 74.
3. Have students repeat the conversation sentence by sentence, and then practice in pairs.

2. WHAT CAN YOU SAY?

Vocabulary

occupations: *sewing machine operator, baker, factory worker, cashier, janitor, delivery person*

Step-by-Step

1. Ask students to look at the pictures and say any words they can read or guess. Use the board or OHP and write each occupation as it is volunteered in a place corresponding to its location on the page. After you write each occupation, say it, and have students point to it in their books and repeat. Add any occupations students have not volunteered and ask for additional ones that students know.
2. Ask a volunteer to stand and hold up the book for the class to see. (In large classes, make smaller groups with a book held up in each.) Call on one volunteer to say an occupation and another to point to the picture for the class.
3. Have students work in pairs, one saying an occupation and the other pointing. Then have students write the occupations several times, and dictate them to each other in pairs.

Pronunciation

Use Imitation and Correction with *cashier, machine,* and *teacher.* (See page xi.) The middle consonant in *teacher* has a momentary complete stoppage before the friction begins, unlike the other two words. Ask students to add words that fit these two categories.

Cross-Reference

The New Oxford Picture Dictionary: Occupations I, II, and III, pages 84–86

3. TALK ABOUT JOB OPENINGS. USE THE CONVERSATION IN 1. USE THE JOBS IN 2.

Competency

[a] Ask about job openings.

Step-by-Step

1. Write the conversation from Exercise 1 on the board or OHP without filling in *sewing machine operators.* Show students that the information for the blank comes from Exercise 2. Fill in the blank with the example.
2. Read the conversation aloud and have students repeat. Then have them repeat the occupations in Exercise 2, including the jobs students added to the list. Have pairs of students say the conversation for the class until all the occupations have been used.
3. Have students practice in pairs, changing partners, saying both parts, and using all the words in Exercise 2.

NOTE: If the applicant asks *Do you have any openings for sewing machine operators?* and the secretary replies *No, we don't,* the applicant can say *Can I fill out an application for the future?*

4. PRACTICE.

Grammar

can: affirmative and negative statements; *yes/no* questions; *yes/no* short answers

Step-by-Step

1. Have students close their books. Play the tape or read the conversation aloud, indicating which character is speaking each line.
2. Have students say anything they can recall of the conversation. Acknowledge all contributions by restating them in acceptable English.
3. Play the tape while students follow along in their books. Then elicit or demonstrate the meaning of *interview* and *Can you come for an interview at 10:00 tomorrow?* Play the tape as many times as students need.
4. Have students repeat the conversation sentence by sentence, and practice in pairs.

NOTE: Emphasize the importance of being polite to the secretary who often initially screens job applicants.

Cross-Reference

Multilevel Activity and Resource Package: Go Fish

5. FOCUS ON GRAMMAR.

Grammar

can: affirmative and negative statements; *yes/no* questions; *yes/no* short answers

Step-by-Step

***can: yes/no* questions; *yes/no* short answers**

1. Have a volunteer read *Can they come in the afternoon?* and *Yes, they can,* or *No, they can't.* Write them on the board side by side, read them, and have students repeat.
2. Write *she* in all three columns, elicit the question and answers. Write them on the board, read them, and have students repeat.
3. Repeat Steps 1 and 2 with *we, he,* and *they,* eliciting questions and answers. Underline *can* and *come.* Elicit that *can* has the same form for all pronouns. Underline *can't.* Elicit that *can not* contracts to *can't.*
4. Write *Can he speak English?* in the first column and elicit *Yes, he can,* or *No, he can't.* Elicit other examples, write them, read them, and have students repeat. Have students write their own sentences, and have volunteers put them on the board. Correct them with the whole class, read them, and have students repeat.

***can:* affirmative and negative statements; *yes/ no* questions**

5. Write *They can come for an interview* and *can't* in two new columns. Elicit *No, they can't come for an interview* and write it in the second column. Point to *Can he speak English?* and elicit *Yes, he can speak English* and *No, he can't speak English.* Write them in these two columns, read them, and have students repeat. Continue with the sentences that students volunteered in Step 4.
6. Have students copy the sentences on a separate piece of paper, then work in pairs generating new sentences both orally and in writing. Have volunteers write sentences on the board and correct them with the whole class.

NOTE: *Can* is used to express ability (as seen here in most sentences) or permission. *Can you come for an interview at 10:00?* (ability); *I can't come then. Can I come in the morning?* (ability/permission). Clarify the distinction only if students are confused.

Conversations

6. TALK ABOUT APPOINTMENTS. USE ANY TIMES. *(PAGE 75)*

Competency

b Set a time for a job interview.

Grammar

can: affirmative and negative statements; *yes/no* questions; *yes/no* short answers

Step-by-Step

1. Write the conversation on the board or OHP without filling in the handwritten parts. Tell students that any time can be used for the blanks. Fill in the blanks as in the example.
2. Read the conversation aloud and have students repeat. Have pairs of students say the conversation for the class using other times and *morning* or *afternoon* as appropriate.
3. Have students practice in pairs, changing partners, saying both parts, and using different times.

7. PRACTICE.

Grammar

past tense of *be:* affirmative statements
can: affirmative statements

Step-by-Step

1. Have students look at the picture of Sue and Mr. Hill. Encourage them to guess what they are saying now.
2. Have students close their books. Play the tape or read the conversation aloud, indicating which character is speaking each line.
3. Have students say anything they can recall of the conversation. Acknowledge all contributions by restating them in acceptable English.
4. Play the tape while students follow along in their books. Then elicit or demonstrate the meaning of *experience, power machines, Please have a seat,* and *What job are you applying for?* Play the tape as many times as students need.
5. Have students repeat the conversation sentence by sentence, and practice in pairs.

8. TALK ABOUT WORK EXPERIENCE.

Competency

C Answer questions about work experience.

Grammar

past tense of *be:* affirmative statements

Step-by-Step

1. Write the conversation on the board or OHP without filling in the handwritten parts. Show students that the information for the blanks comes from Exercise 2, page 74. Fill in the blanks.
2. Read the conversation aloud and have students repeat. Also have them repeat the occupations in Exercise 2, including those jobs students added to the list. Write the names of countries represented in the class on the board or OHP and review their pronunciation if necessary. Have pairs of students say the conversation with all the occupations and have them replace *Vietnam* with the countries listed on the board until all of them have been used.
3. Have students practice in pairs, changing partners, saying both parts, and using all the occupations in Exercise 2 and the countries.

Conversations

9. PRACTICE. *(PAGE 76)*

Grammar

past tense of *be:* affirmative and negative statements; *yes/no* questions; *yes/no* short answers

Step-by-Step

1. Have students look at the picture of Sue and Mr. Hill who are continuing their conversation.
2. Have students close their books. Play the tape or read the conversation aloud, indicating which character is speaking each line.
3. Have students say anything they can recall of the conversation. Acknowledge all contributions by restating them in acceptable English.
4. Play the tape while students follow along in their books. Then elicit or demonstrate the meaning of *full-time job, part-time, Were you happy with your job?, closed,* and *laid off.* Note the use of the past tense of *be.* Play the tape as many times as students need.
5. Have students repeat the conversation sentence by sentence, and practice in pairs.

Going Further

Have students brainstorm reasons why Sue is having a good interview in Exercises 7 and 9. (She uses complete sentences; she smiles; and when she says she doesn't have experience, she adds something positive to show that she can learn.) Have students make a reference list for their interviews.

10. FOCUS ON GRAMMAR.

Grammar

past tense of *be:* affirmative and negative statements; *yes/no* questions; *yes/no* short answers

Step-by-Step

past tense of *be: yes/no* questions; *yes/no* short answers with adjectives and plural pronouns

1. Have volunteers read *Were you happy?* and *Yes, you were.* Write them in two columns on the board or OHP, read them aloud, and have students repeat. Elicit *No, you weren't,* write it in the third column, read it, and have students repeat.
2. Repeat Step 1 with *we* and *you.* Erase *happy.* Elicit other adjectives (*sad, angry, sick, old, young,* and so on). As each one is suggested, erase the previous word, write it in the sentence, and have students repeat.

past tense of *be: yes/no* questions; *yes/no* short answers with occupations and plural pronouns

3. Erase *Were we happy?* in the first column and replace it with *Were we bakers?* Read it and have students repeat. Erase *bakers.* Elicit other occupations *(cashiers, factory workers, sewing machine operators, janitors,* and so on). As each occupation is suggested, erase the previous one and write it in the sentence, and have students repeat.
4. Point to *you, we, they* and the *-s* ending on the occupations. Elicit that *were* is used for all three pronouns.

past tense of *be: yes/no* questions; *yes/no* short answers with occupations, adjectives, and singular pronouns

5. Repeat Steps 1 to 4 with the singular pronouns *I, he,* and *she,* as well as the adjectives and occupations.
6. Have students work in pairs saying and writing new questions and short answers. Have volunteers write their questions and answers on the board, correct them with the whole class, and have students copy them.

NOTE: *You* takes *were,* but may be either singular or plural. *(Were you a janitor?, Were you janitors?)*

Going Further

Drill singular/plural and question/answer.

T: *We were bakers.*
S: *We were bakers.*
T: *He.*
T: *Question.*
S: *He was a baker.*
S: *Was he a baker?*
etc.

Option

BEFORE  CLASS

Using the *Multilevel Activity and Resource Package* Word Cards, scramble sentences using all forms of *be* in the past tense and have students unscramble them.

11. TALK ABOUT THE PEOPLE.

Grammar

past tense of *be:* affirmative and negative statements; *yes/no* questions; *yes/no* short answers

Step-by-Step

1. Write the conversation on the board or OHP without filling in the handwritten parts. Show students that the information for the blanks comes from illustrations and cues below. Fill in the blanks.
2. Read the conversation aloud and have students repeat. Also have them repeat the occupations and countries. Have pairs of students say the conversation for the class until all the occupations and countries have been used.
3. Have students practice in pairs, changing partners, saying both parts, and using all the occupations and countries.

Option

If possible, have students talk about their classmates' former occupations.

Pronunciation

Use Imitation and Correction with *janitor, job, Japan, yes,* and *you,* which pose problems for students from many language backgrounds. (See page xi.) For /j/, the tongue must make momentary complete stoppage against the hard, bony part of the roof of the mouth, followed by audible turbulence (friction) as the breath escapes. For /y/, the tongue must be kept far enough away from the roof of the mouth that no audible turbulence is generated. Ask students to add words to both lists.

Cross-Reference

Multilevel Activity and Resource Package: Grammar and Word Tap

Paperwork

1. READ RAMONA'S APPLICATION. *(PAGE 77)*

Vocabulary on forms

Are you legally able to be employed in the U.S.?, U.S. citizen?, Date available?, What shifts can you work?

Step-by-Step

1. Draw an outline of the application form on the board or OHP.
2. Have volunteers say any words from the form that they can read or guess. As each word is said, write it on the form on the board, say it aloud, and have students repeat.
3. Elicit or supply missing items in the same way.
4. Elicit or demonstrate the meaning of words on the form by asking questions about Ramona. *(Is Ramona legally able to be employed in the U.S.? Is she a U.S. citizen?)*
5. Point to items in the completed form at random and have students read them aloud. Leave the form on the board.

NOTE: People with tourist or student visas, as well as illegal immigrants, cannot work legally in the U.S.

Option

Elicit other words for work shifts (first = regular/day; second = evening/swing; third = night/graveyard).

2. FILL OUT THE JOB APPLICATION.

Competency

[d] Fill out a simple job application form.

Step-by-Step

1. Use the form on the board. Erase Ramona's information in the form and fill it in one blank at a time with information about yourself. Make statements with the information.
2. Erase your information, interview a volunteer, and fill in the form. Leave the filled-in form on the board for students to use as a model.
3. Have students fill in the forms in their books with their own information. Provide assistance when necessary. Have students check each other's answers in pairs.

3. INTERVIEW THREE CLASSMATES.

Competency

[e] Answer questions about work shifts, hours, and starting dates.

Step-by-Step

1. Copy the interview questions on the board or OHP and have students repeat them.
2. Invite a student to speak for Ramona. Interview "Ramona" and fill in her answers with students' help. Erase her answers.
3. Have a volunteer interview you and write your answers on the board. Correct the answers with the whole class.
4. Have students ask three classmates the questions and write their answers on a separate piece of paper.

Going Further

Have students ask other questions during the interview. *(What is your first name? What is your ZIP code?)*

Cross-Reference

Multilevel Activity and Resource Package: Picture Story and Concentration

Reading and Writing

1. WHAT CAN YOU SAY ABOUT THE JOB NOTICE? *(PAGE 78)*

Pre-reading.

Step-by-Step

1. Have students look at the job notice and the picture of the hospital worker. Have them say anything they can. As each word, phrase, or sentence is suggested, write it on the board or OHP, say it, and have students repeat.
2. Add any key phrases from the reading that students have not volunteered *(openings, take care of, The job pays $6.00 an hour,* and *in the future)*. Point to items at random and have students read them aloud.

2. READ ABOUT YOUNG HO.

Reading stories.

Step-by-Step

1. Give students time to look at the story and read what they can. Then play the tape or read the story aloud while students follow in their books.
2. Play the tape one sentence at a time and have students repeat. Then have volunteers read sentences of the story aloud.

Option

Choose a word from the reading, such as *full-time,* and give a synonym or a simple definition *(forty hours a week)*. Ask students to point to the word or phrase in their books which has the same meaning, and have a volunteer read it aloud.

3. ANSWER THE QUESTIONS ON A SEPARATE PIECE OF PAPER.

Comprehension check.

Step-by-Step

1. Write *What does Young Ho do?* on the board or OHP. Elicit the answer *(Young Ho is a factory worker)*, and write it next to the question.
2. Have students work in pairs, answering the questions in their books.
3. Write the questions on the board as volunteers read each one aloud. Have volunteers write the answers on the board next to each question. Have the class correct the sentences and check their work.

Pronunciation

Use the Human Computer™ with the questions and answers on the board. (See page xii.)

Going Further

Have students rewrite the answers using Young Ho and his brother.

Cross-Reference

Multilevel Activity and Resource Package: Listening and Game: Job Search

Reading and Writing

4. IMAGINE THAT YOU NEED A JOB. ANSWER THESE QUESTIONS. *(PAGE 79)*

Pre-writing.

Step-by-Step

1. Write the questions on the board or OHP. Say them and have students repeat.
2. Have a student interview you and write your answers on the board in the appropriate place. Use realistic, yet fictional information.
3. Correct the answers with the whole class. Leave them on the board.
4. Have students write their answers in their books. Circulate and answer any questions. Have students compare answers.

5. WRITE A JOB NOTICE FOR A JOB YOU WANT. USE YOUR ANSWERS IN 4.

Writing a job notice.

Step-by-Step

1. Reproduce the job notice on the board or OHP without filling in the blanks.
2. Refer students to your answers in Exercise 4. Fill in the blanks in the job notice with students' help. Leave it on the board as a model.
3. Have students fill in the job notice in their books using their answers in Exercise 4. Have them compare job notices with several other students.

6. ANSWER THE QUESTIONS.

Pre-writing.

Step-by-Step

1. Have volunteers read each question as you write it on the board or OHP. Answer each question in a complete sentence, and write it on the board. Read each sentence and have students repeat. Leave the sentences on the board as a model.
2. Have students answer the questions in their books. Circulate to help as needed. Have volunteers read their answers aloud.

Option

Add other questions to the list. *(What is your job now? What are your hours? Do you like your job?)*

7. WRITE A STORY ABOUT YOURSELF. USE YOUR ANSWERS IN 4 AND 6.

Multi-sentence writing.

Step-by-Step

1. Tell your story to the class based on your answers in Exercises 4 and 6. Use Young Ho's story on page 78 as a model. Help students restate what you have said to confirm their understanding.
2. Write your story on the board or OHP. Leave it on the board as a model.
3. Have students work in pairs, telling their stories to each other, restating them, and changing roles.
4. Have students write their stories. Encourage them to help each other. Circulate to give help as needed or to listen to students' stories.

Option

After Step 2, have students interview a volunteer and create a story based on the volunteer's information. Write their sentences on the board or OHP just as students dictate them. Then have the class correct them.

8. READ YOUR STORY TO YOUR GROUP.

Lets students share their writing.

Step-by-Step

1. Have a volunteer read her story to the class. Lead the class in applause.
2. Have the class restate the story to confirm understanding. Have the volunteer clarify meaning, if necessary.
3. Have students work in groups to read their stories in turn and to receive applause and responses from their peers.
4. Have students copy their stories. Publish them by posting them in the classroom.

Cross-Reference

Multilevel Activity and Resource Package: Writing and Question Game

Listening Plus

1. WHAT'S NEXT? *(PAGE 80)*

Predicting with social and grammatical clues.

Step-by-Step

1. Have students close their books. Write the first response for *a* on the board or OHP. Read it aloud and have students repeat.
2. Have students work in pairs to guess what might come before.
3. Have pairs volunteer their ideas. Help the class evaluate each one.
4. Do the same with the other responses in *a*. Leave the responses on the board.
5. Have students open their books and have a volunteer come to the board.
6. Play the tape or read the tapescript aloud one conversation at a time. Have students point to the correct response in their books and have the volunteer point to it at the board. Play the tape as many times as students need.
7. Repeat the process for *b*.

2. REVIEW...WRITE...NUMBER.

Focused listening.

ANSWER KEY

Write: a. *$6.35/11:30 p.m. to 7:30 a.m.;* b. *$8.50/4 a.m. to noon, 4 days;* c. *$4.25/3:30 p.m. to 11:30 p.m.;* d. *$3.75/Fridays and Saturdays, 4 p.m. to midnight;* e. *$4.50/6 p.m. to 2 a.m.;* f. *$4.50/6 a.m. to 2 p.m.*

Number: a. *4;* b. *1;* c. *5;* d. *2;* e. *6;* f. *3*

REVIEW.

Step-by-Step

1. Have students look at the ads and read or say anything they can about them. Acknowledge all contributions by restating them in acceptable English.
2. As vocabulary from the unit is volunteered, write it on the board or OHP, say it, and have students repeat.
3. Elicit any other vocabulary which will be helpful in distinguishing among the items.
4. Point to items on the board at random and have volunteers read them aloud.

WRITE.

Step-by-Step

1. Copy the answer blanks on the board or OHP.
2. Play the tape or read the first conversation aloud. Fill in the first answer as students hear it.
3. Continue playing the tape one conversation at a time and have students fill in the other pay and hours. Play the tape as many times as students need.
4. Have students compare their answers in pairs.
5. Play the tape again, one conversation at a time. Have a volunteer write the answers on the board. Correct the student's answers with the whole class.
6. Have students check their answers against the answers on the board, then play the tape once more so that students can verify their answers.

NUMBER.

Step-by-Step

1. Play the tape or read the tapescript aloud one conversation at a time, as many times as students need. Have students number the ads in the order of the conversations they hear.

2. Have students compare their answers in pairs.
3. Play the tape again and have a volunteer write the answers on the board. Correct any errors with the whole class.
4. Have students check their answers against the answers on the board, then play the tape once more so that students can verify their answers.

3. A, TELL ABOUT THE JOBS IN 2. B, SAY WHAT YOU HEARD AND POINT.

Speaking and active listening.

Step-by-Step

1. Have volunteers make statements about one of the jobs in Exercise 2. Repeat each statement. Demonstrate the use of clarification strategies (for example, *How much?, How many?,* or *What job?).*
2. Have students hold up their books and point to the job described.
3. Have students work in pairs to make statements, restate, and point. Each student should change partners and describe all the jobs. Circulate to listen and give help as needed.

4. WHAT ABOUT YOU?

Listening and responding with personal information.

Step-by-Step

1. Play the tape once. Have students confer in groups to reconstruct the statement they heard. Circulate to hear what they say.
2. Repeat Step 1 until most groups have the gist of the statement.
3. Have groups share their reconstructions and help them reach a consensus.
4. Play the tape again so that students can verify their reconstruction.
5. Have students answer the question on the tape by writing similar information about themselves. Encourage students to vary or extend their answers. Circulate to give help and feedback.
6. Have several volunteers put their answers on the board. Help volunteers extend their answers if they have not already done so. Correct any errors with the whole class.
7. Have students compare their own answers with the answers on the board, then check each other's answers in pairs.

Cross-Reference

Multilevel Activity and Resource Package: Categories

Interactions

1. & 2. GET INFORMATION/GIVE INFORMATION. *(PAGES 81 AND 82)*

Information gap for communicative practice.

Step-by-Step

1. Write the conversation on the board or OHP without filling in the handwritten parts. Review the vocabulary on the application form, if necessary, by having students ask questions about Ramona's application form, Exercise 1, page 77. *(What is Ramona's Social Security number? When can she start work?)* Write *Citizenship* and *What job are you applying for?* on the board or OHP. Elicit the corresponding questions. *(What is her citizenship?* and *What job is she applying for?)*
2. Divide the class into a Student A group and a Student B group, and have them open their books to their group's page. Have the A group point to the blanks on their form and the B group point to the complete form. Then have students switch roles for Rashid's form.
3. Fill in the conversation, read it aloud sentence by sentence, and have students repeat. Take B's part and have a volunteer take A's part.
4. Have volunteers from both groups say the conversation. Erase the information in the blanks. Call on new volunteers to say the conversation using *Elena's social security number.* Fill in the blanks.
5. Have students work in pairs to fill in their applications. Each student should change partners and do both pages.

Cross-Reference

Multilevel Activity and Resource Package: Jigsaw Reading

Progress Checks

1. FILL OUT THE APPLICATION. *(PAGE 83)*

Competency

[d] Fill out a simple job application form.

2. WHAT ARE THE PEOPLE SAYING?/ DO IT YOURSELF.

Competencies

[a] Ask about job openings.

[b] Set a time for a job interview.

Basic Conversation

A: *Do you have any openings for factory workers?*
B: *Yes, we do.*
A: *Can you come for an interview tomorrow afternoon?*
B: *I'm sorry. I can't. Can I come in the morning?*
A: *Yes. Come at 10:00.*

In *Do It Yourself,* have students ask about jobs they would like to have. Have each student write out her schedule for the next week before the exercise so that they can actually negotiate an appointment.

Progress Checks

3. WHAT ARE THEY SAYING?/ DO IT YOURSELF. *(PAGE 84)*

Competencies

[c] Answer questions about work experience.

[e] Answer questions about work shifts, hours, and starting dates.

Basic Conversation

A: *What job are you applying for?*
B: *Cashier.*
A: *Do you have any experience?*
B: *Yes. I was a cashier in Mexico.*
A: *Can you work full-time?*
B: *No, part-time.*
A: *What hours can you work?*
B: *From 4:00 p.m. to 8:00 p.m.*
A: *When can you start?*
B: *Next Monday.*

In *Do It Yourself,* have students apply for jobs they would like to have and answer with their own information.

Going Further

Have students apply for jobs for which they have no experience. Have them answer the interviewer's second question with *No, I don't, but I can learn,* or *No, I don't, but I'm very good with math,* and so on.

Memo to the Teacher

Option

Have groups of students prepare dialogues for a successful or an unsuccessful interview. Have pairs of students perform them for the class.

UNIT

8 On the Job

COMPETENCIES

State a need for tools • Give simple excuses for lateness or absence • Ask to cash a check or money order • Show proper ID • Apologize for forgetting something • Endorse a check or money order • Follow spoken instructions about where to put things

GRAMMAR

me, you, him, her, it, us, them
past tense of *be: wh-* questions
to the left/right, on the bottom/top/middle, at, under (location)

Warm-ups

1. Hangman (Use at any point in the unit.)
Choose a familiar word and draw blanks for each letter on the board or OHP. Draw a simple gallows next to the blanks. Each student has one chance to guess a letter. If the guess is correct, write the letter in the blank(s). If it's incorrect, draw one part of the hanged man's body. The game ends when someone guesses the word, or when the hanged man is complete.

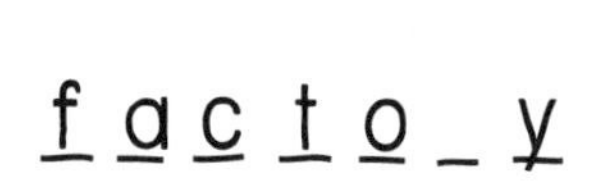

BEFORE

CLASS

2. Charades (Use after page 86.)
Use picture cards of tools from the *Multilevel Activity and Resource Package* or make your own cards. Divide the class into two teams. Put the cards face down and let a volunteer from one team take a card. The player has six seconds to mime using the tool so that his teammates can guess its name. If they guess it, give the team a point and retire the card. If they cannot guess it correctly within six seconds, the player puts the card back into the pile.

BEFORE

CLASS

3. Picture Grids (Use after page 90.)
Have students work in pairs. First, give each student a grid made by dividing a sheet of paper into ten equal rectangles (two vertical columns of five). Give students identical sets of ten word cards or picture cards of tools from the *Multilevel Activity and Resource Package,* or have students make their own cards. Student A places cards on each rectangle of his grid, without letting his partner see them. Student B asks questions in order to put her cards on her grid in the same position as A's. *(Where's the hammer? It's in the top row to the left of the screwdriver.)* When all of B's cards are in place, they compare their grids, and then change roles.

Getting Started

1. GUESS. *(PAGE 85)*

Establishes the context of the unit.

Step-by-Step

1. Have students look at the pictures of Antonio and John and ask where they are.
2. Remind students that Antonio is a student and encourage them to guess that John is his co-worker.
3. Ask students to guess what Antonio and John are saying. All responses are valid here. Respond to each guess by restating it in acceptable English.

2. WHAT CAN YOU HEAR?

Prepares students to read the first conversation on page 86.

Step-by-Step

1. Have students look at the pictures while you play the tape or read the tapescript aloud.
2. Have students volunteer any words or sentences they can recall from the conversation. Acknowledge all contributions by restating them in acceptable English.
3. Let students hear the conversation again to elicit more of it.

Conversations

1. PRACTICE. *(PAGE 86)*

Grammar

past tense of *be*
him, it, them
under, on (location)

Step-by-Step

1. Play the tape or read the conversation while students follow along in their books.
2. Elicit or demonstrate the meaning of *scissors, them, Never mind, under the table, screw driver, Hmm, maybe, it, on the pegboard,* and *him.* Play the tape as many times as students need.
3. Have students repeat the conversation sentence by sentence, and then practice in pairs.

2. WHAT CAN YOU SAY?

Vocabulary

tools: *hammer, scissors, screwdriver, pliers, wrench, tape measure, nails, extension cord, screws, saw*

Step-by-Step

1. Ask students to look at the pictures and say any words they can read or guess. Use the board or OHP and write each tool as it is volunteered in a place corresponding to its location on the page. After you write each tool, say it, and have students point to it in their books and repeat. Add any words students have not volunteered.
2. Ask a volunteer to stand and hold up the book for the class to see. (In large classes, make smaller groups with a book held up in each.) Call on one volunteer to say a tool and another to point to the picture for the class.
3. Have students work in pairs, one saying a tool and the other pointing. Then have students write the tools several times and dictate them to each other in pairs.

Option

Have students add other tools to the list. Have them play Concentration with the Word Cards and Picture Cards from the *Multilevel Activity and Resource Package.*

NOTE: *Scissors* and *pliers* are always plural and take the plural form of the verb. We can say *the scissors* or *a pair of scissors,* but not *a scissor.*

Cross-Reference

The New Oxford Picture Dictionary: A Workshop, pages 36 and 37.

3. FOCUS ON GRAMMAR.

Grammar

me, you, him, her, it, us, them

Step-by-Step

***me, you, him, her, it, us, them* in affirmative sentences**

1. Write *I was in the room* and *John saw me* in two columns on the board or OHP. Point to *I* and *me* so that students see the relationship between the subject and object forms. Read the two sentences aloud and have students repeat. Write *you* on the board and elicit *You were in the room* and *John saw you.* Point to *you* in both sentences, read them, and have students repeat.
2. Repeat Step 1 for all the other pronoun forms. Then drill the direct object pronouns by saying a sentence in the left column and having a volunteer say the corresponding right-hand sentence.

***him, her* in imperative sentences**

3. Write *Ask Bill* and *Ask him* in two new columns. Point to *Bill* and *him,* read the two sentences, and have students repeat. Write *Ask Betty* in the first column, elicit *Ask her,* and write it in the second column. Point to *Betty* and *her,* read the two sentences aloud, and have students repeat.
4. Write *Tell him* and *Show her* in the right column and elicit corresponding sentences with a man and a woman's name, write them in the left column, read them, and have students repeat.

***it, them* in affirmative sentences**

5. In two new columns write *Bill took the screwdriver* and *Bill took it* on the board or OHP. Point to *screwdriver* and *it,* read the two sentences aloud, and have students repeat. Continue with *Bill took the scissors* and *Bill took them.* Write *Maria bought it* and *Pablo needed some screws* in the appropriate columns and elicit the corresponding sentences.
6. Drill object pronouns by saying a sentence in the left column and having volunteers say the corresponding sentence in the right column. Then have students work in pairs generating other sentences orally and in writing. Have volunteers write their sentences on the board, correct errors with the whole class, and call on volunteers to read sentences.

4. TALK ABOUT THE TOOLS IN 2.

Competency

a State a need for tools.

Grammar

me, you, him, her, it, us, them

Step-by-Step

1. Write the conversation on the board or OHP without filling in the handwritten parts. Show students that the information for the blanks comes from Exercise 2 and fill them in. Elicit the references to *it (the hammer)* and *them (Ray and Van)* in the conversation.
2. Read the conversation sentence by sentence and have students repeat. Also have them repeat the list of tools in Exercise 2 and the people's names in Exercise 4. Have pairs of students say the conversation with the class until all the tools and names have been used.
3. Have students practice in pairs, changing partners, saying both parts, and using all the tools in Exercise 2 and the people's names in Exercise 4.

Conversations

5. PRACTICE. *(PAGE 87)*

Grammar

past tense of *be: wh-* questions

Step-by-Step

1. Have students look at the picture of Antonio and Mr. Ross and ask where they are. Have students guess that Mr. Ross is Antonio's boss. Then have students guess what they are saying.
2. Have students close their books. Play the tape or read the conversation aloud. Use stick figures to indicate which character is speaking each line.
3. Have students say anything they can recall of the conversation. Acknowledge all contributions by restating them in acceptable English.
4. Play the tape while students follow along in their books. Then elicit or demonstrate the meaning of *Where were you yesterday?, next time, I'm really sorry, I was worried, I forgot,* and *How is your son now?* Play the tape as many times as students need.
5. Have students repeat the conversation sentence by sentence and practice in pairs.

Going Further

Elicit why Mr. Ross said *OK, but call me next time* when Antonio told him he took his son to the doctor and couldn't come to work. Elicit what employees must do or say to their employer when they are late or absent. List helpful ideas on the board or OHP.

Pronunciation

Use Imitation and Correction with *work, worried, were,* and *first.* (See page xi.) The vowel in these words is spelled in different ways and many students find it difficult to pronounce. For English speakers who drop their *r's,* this vowel is formed with the tongue neither high nor low in the mouth, and neither fronted nor backed. English speakers who do not drop their *r's* make this sound by curling up the tip of the tongue slightly.

6. FOCUS ON GRAMMAR.

Grammar

past tense of *be: wh-* questions

Step-by-Step

past tense of *be: wh-* questions with *they, you, we*

1. Have volunteers read *Where were they last night?* and *They were at home.* Write them side by side on the board or OHP, read them, and have students repeat.
2. Underline *Where* and *at home.* Elicit that *where* refers to a place *(at home)*.
3. Write *you* in the first column and elicit *Where were you last night?* and *You were at home.* Write them, read them, and have students repeat. Continue with *we.*

past tense of *be: wh-* questions with *I, he, she, it*

4. Write *he* and *this morning* in the first column and elicit *Where was he this morning?* and *He was at home.* Write the sentences, read them, and have students repeat. Continue with *she, it,* and *I.*
5. Erase *home* in two sentences and replace it with *school* and *work.* Ask questions with different pronouns and different past time phrases and have students answer using any one of the place

phrases. *(Where was she last night? She was at school/Where were they yesterday? They were at work.)*

6. Have students work in pairs, saying and writing other sentences. Have volunteers write their sentences on the board, correct them with the whole class, and have students copy them.

Option

Have students create questions and answers using *where* and the past tense of *be* with Word Cards from the *Multilevel Activity and Resource Package.*

7. WHAT CAN YOU SAY?

Vocabulary

excuses: *I was sick, My babysitter didn't come, My car broke down.*

Step-by-Step

1. Ask students to look at the pictures and say any words they can read or guess. Use the board or OHP and write each excuse as it is volunteered in a place corresponding to its location on the page. After you write each excuse, say it, and have students point to it in their books and repeat. Add any words students have not volunteered.
2. Ask a volunteer to stand and hold up the book for the class to see. (In large classes, make smaller groups with a book held up in each.) Call on one volunteer to say an excuse and another to point to the picture for the class.
3. Have students work in pairs, one saying an excuse and the other pointing. Then have students write the excuses several times, and dictate them to each other in pairs.

Going Further

Have students add other reasons for being late to or absent from work or school. *(My wife had a doctor's appointment. I had to take her to the clinic. My brother arrived at the airport. I had to meet him.)* Contrast the difference between absence and lateness. Elicit ways to present each reason to one's boss or teacher in an appropriate and diplomatic way.

8. TALK ABOUT LATENESS OR ABSENCE. USE THE EXCUSES IN 7.

Competency

b Give simple excuses for lateness or absence.

Step-by-Step

1. Write the conversation on the board or OHP without filling in the handwritten parts. Show students that the information for the blanks come from Exercise 7. Fill in the blanks.
2. Read the conversation aloud and have students repeat. Also have them repeat the words in Exercise 7. Have pairs of students say the conversation for the class until all the excuses have been used.
3. Have students practice in pairs, changing partners, saying both parts, and using all the excuses in Exercise 7.

Cross-Reference

Multilevel Activity and Resource Package: Go Fish, Grammar, Strip Story, and Writing

Conversations

9. PRACTICE. *(PAGE 88)*

Vocabulary

a bank teller, to cash a check, identification, to endorse a check, Sorry, No problem

Step-by-Step

1. Have students look at the picture and identify Antonio and the bank teller. Encourage them to guess what Antonio and the bank teller are saying.
2. Have students close their books. Play the tape or read the conversation aloud, indicating which character is speaking each line.
3. Have students say anything they can recall of the conversation. Acknowledge all contributions by restating them in acceptable English.
4. Play the tape while students follow along in their books. Then elicit or demonstrate the meaning of any key words, phrases, or sentences. Play the tape as many times as students need.
5. Have students repeat the conversation sentence by sentence, and practice in pairs.

10. WHAT CAN YOU SAY?

Vocabulary

a check, a money order

Step-by-Step

1. Ask students to look at the pictures and say any words they can read or guess. Use the board or OHP and write each word as it is volunteered in a place corresponding to its location on the page. After you write each word, say it, and have students point to it in their books and repeat. Add any words students have not volunteered.
2. Ask a volunteer to stand and hold up the book for the class to see. (In large classes, make smaller groups with a book held up in each.) Call on one volunteer to say a word and another to point to the picture.
3. Have students work in pairs, one saying a word and the other pointing. Then have students write each word several times and dictate the words to each other in pairs.

Option

BEFORE

CLASS

Bring in actual checks, money orders, ID cards, or driver's licenses to illustrate the words, or make facsimilies and hand them out. Say *Show me a driver's license,* for example, and have students hold up that item.

11. TALK ABOUT GETTING CASH.

Competencies

c Ask to cash a check or money order.

d Show proper ID.

e Apologize for forgetting something.

f Endorse a check or money order.

Step-by-Step

BEFORE

CLASS

1. Say and then demonstrate the instructions *Can you cash this check, please?, Do you have any identification?,* and *endorse your check* by handing out a sample check and having students follow the instructions.
2. Write the conversation on the board or OHP without filling in the handwritten parts. Show students that the information for the blanks comes from Exercise 10. Fill in the blanks.
3. Read the conversation aloud and have students repeat. Also have them repeat the words in Exercise 10. Have pairs of students say the conversation for the class until all the words have been used.
4. Have students practice in pairs, changing partners, saying both parts, and using all the words in Exercise 10 in all possible combinations.

Going Further

Elicit other ways to say *No problem. (That's okay, Don't worry about it.)* Have students use them as alternatives in the conversation.

Cross-Reference

Multilevel Activity and Resource Package: Scrambled Sentences, Picture Story, and Word Tap

Paperwork

1. READ ANTONIO'S PAYCHECK. *(PAGE 89)*

Reading paychecks.

Step-by-Step

1. Draw two outlines of the paycheck onthe board or OHP, one for the front and one for the back of the paycheck.
2. Have volunteers say any words or phrases from the paycheck they can read or guess. As each word is said, write it on the paycheck on the board, say it aloud, and have students repeat.
3. Elicit or supply missing items in the same way.
4. Elicit or demonstrate the meaning of the words on the paycheck by asking questions about Antonio. *(What is the name of Antonio's company?* or *Did Antonio endorse his check?)*
5. Point to items in the completed paycheck at random and have students read them aloud. Leave the check on the board.

2. HOW MUCH DOES ANTONIO MAKE EVERY WEEK?

Comprehension check.

Step-by-Step

1. Have students look at the sentences in the direction line in Exercise 1 and read what they can. Read them aloud while students follow along silently.
2. Write *How much does Antonio make every week?* on the board or OHP. Elicit the meaning of *make*. Ask students to solve the problem (multiplying 40 x $5.75 = $230). Have volunteers read their answer. Write it on the board and have students copy it.
3. Write *What's his take-home pay?* on the board or OHP. Elicit the meaning of *take-home* and the answer to the question *($208.70)*. Ask students to point to the answer in their books. Write the answer on the board and have students copy it.

Going Further

Ask students why the *take-home pay* is less than Antonio's weekly earnings. Elicit that federal, state, and local taxes, as well as Social Security, are withheld from everyone's paycheck in order to provide government services.

3. INTERVIEW THREE CLASSMATES.

Speaking and writing.

Step-by-Step

1. Write the questions on the board or OHP, without filling in Antonio's information.
2. Say the interview questions one at a time and have students repeat them.
3. Invite a student to speak for Antonio. Interview "Antonio" and fill in the form with students' help.
4. Have a volunteer interview you and write your answers on the board. Correct the answers with the whole class.
5. Have students ask and answer the questions with three classmates and write their answers on a separate piece of paper.

Going Further

Have students add other questions *(How much do you make every week?*, or *Where do you work?)*. Allow students to use fictitious information if they wish.

Cross-Reference

Multilevel Activity and Resource Package: Categories

Reading and Writing

1. WHAT CAN YOU SAY ABOUT THE TOOLS ON THIS WORKTABLE? *(PAGE 90)*

Grammar

to the left of, to the right of, on (location)

Step-by-Step

1. Have students look at the picture and say anything they can read or guess. As each word, phrase, or sentence is suggested, write it on the board or OHP in a place corresponding to its location in the exercise, say it, and have students repeat.
2. Add any key phrase from the list in Exercise 2 that students have not volunteered. Point to items at random and have students read them aloud.

Going Further

Draw a rough sketch of the shelves, pegboard, and worktable in Exercise 1 on the board. Include the screwdriver, tape measure, hammer, wrench, and saw. Put an *X* in different places on the diagram and ask *Where is it?* Elicit phrases of location *(on the pegboard,* or *to the right of the hammer)*.

2. READ THE LIST.

Reading.

Step-by-Step

1. Read the direction line while students follow in their books. Elicit the meaning of *put the tools away, storeroom,* and *list.*
2. Give students time to look at the list and read what they can. Play the tape or read the list while students follow in their books.
3. Play the tape one line at a time (including just one tool and its location) and have students repeat. Then have volunteers read lines aloud.

Cross-Reference

Multilevel Activity and Resource Package: Listening and Concentration

Reading and Writing

3. WHAT TOOLS DID JOHN PUT IN THE WRONG PLACE? *(PAGE 91)*

Comprehension check.

Step-by-Step

1. Have students look at the picture. Elicit the location of each tool. *(Where is the saw? Where are the scissors?)* Write their answers on the board or OHP, read them, and have students repeat.
2. Have students look at the list in Exercise 2 and compare the locations in the list with the locations in this exercise. Have them circle the tools that are in the *wrong* place (tape measure, hammer, saw, scissors, screws, and extension cord). Then have them write the names of the tools where the tools are supposed to be. Have them compare their answers in pairs.
3. Have volunteers answer the question *What tools did John put in the wrong place? (John put the extension cord in the wrong place. He didn't put it on the shelf under the pegboard. He put it on the bottom shelf.)*

Option

Have volunteers write their answers from Step 3 on the board. Check their work and leave it on the board as a model. Have students copy the sentences on a separate piece of paper.

4. IMAGINE THAT YOUR ARE MR. ROSS. WRITE A NOTE TO JOHN.

Multi-sentence writing.

Step-by-Step

1. Have students look at Mr. Ross' note to John and read the first two sentences. Write the sentences on the board or OHP. Show students that the instructions in the note come from the list in Exercise 2.
2. Have students write the rest of the note and include instructions for all six tools that were put in the wrong place.

5. SHOW YOUR NOTE TO YOUR PARTNER.

Lets students share their writing and check their comprehension.

Step-by-Step

1. Have pairs of students compare their notes and make any corrections they can.
2. Have volunteers write sentences from their notes on the board. Correct them with the whole class, and have volunteers read them aloud.

Cross-Reference

Multilevel Activity and Resource Package: Game: Test Your Memory and Game: Tools on the Worktable

Listening Plus

1. WHAT'S NEXT? *(PAGE 92)*

Predicting with social and grammatical clues.

Step-by-Step

1. Have students close their books. Write the first response for *a* on the board or OHP. Read it aloud and have students repeat.
2. Have students work in pairs to guess what might come before.
3. Have pairs volunteer their ideas. Help the class evaluate each one.
4. Do the same with the other responses in *a*. Leave the responses on the board.
5. Have students open their books and have a volunteer come to the board.
6. Play the tape or read the tapescript aloud one conversation at a time. Have students point to the correct response in their books and have the volunteer point to it at the board. Play the tape as many times as students need.
7. Repeat the process for *b*.

2. REVIEW...WRITE...NUMBER.

Focused listening.

ANSWER KEY

Write: b. *tape measure* (on the floor under the table); c. *pliers* (on the table, to the left of the screwdriver); d. *wrench* (on the bottom shelf, next to the extension cord); e. *saw* (on the wastebasket); f. *nails* (on the middle shelf)

Number: 1. *pliers;* 2. *wastebasket;* 3. *scissors;* 4. *screws;* 5. *extension cord;* 6. *hammer*

REVIEW.

Step-by-Step

1. Have students look at the picture and say anything they can about it. Acknowledge all contributions by restating them in acceptable English.
2. As vocabulary needed for *Write* is volunteered, write it on the board or OHP, say it, and have students repeat.
3. Elicit any other vocabulary which will be helpful in distinguishing among the items.
4. Point to items on the board at random and have volunteers read them aloud.

WRITE.

Step-by-Step

1. Copy the picture on the board or OHP.
2. Play the tape or read the first conversation aloud. Write the name of the first tool *(hammer)* as students hear it.
3. Continue playing the tape one conversation at a time and have students fill in the other tools. Play the tape as many times as students need.
4. Have students compare their answers in pairs.
5. Play the tape again, one conversation at a time. Have a volunteer write the answers on the board. Correct the answers with the whole class.
6. Have students check their answers against the answers on the board, then play the tape once more so that students can verify their answers.

NUMBER.

Step-by-Step

1. Play the tape or read the tapescript aloud one conversation at a time, as many times as students need. Have students number the tools in the order of the conversations they hear.
2. Have students compare their answers in pairs.
3. Play the tape again and have a volunteer write the answers on the board. Correct any errors with the whole class.
4. Have students check their answers against the answers on the board, then play the tape once more so that students can verify their answers.

3. A, GIVE THE LOCATION OF SOMETHING IN 2. B, SAY WHAT YOU HEARD AND POINT.

Speaking and active listening.

Step-by-Step

1. Have volunteers make statements about one of the tools in Exercise 2. Repeat each statement. Demonstrate the use of clarification strategies (for example, *Where?*, *What?*, or *Which tool?*).
2. Have students hold up their books and point to the location described.
3. Have students work in pairs to make statements, restate, and point. Each student should change partners and describe all the locations. Circulate to listen and give help as needed.

4. WHAT ABOUT YOU?

Listening and responding with personal information.

Step-by-Step

1. Play the tape once. Have students confer in groups to reconstruct the statement they heard. Circulate to hear what they say.
2. Repeat Step 1 until most groups have the gist of the statement.
3. Have groups share their reconstructions and help them reach a consensus.
4. Play the tape again so that students can verify their reconstruction.
5. Have students answer the question on the tape by writing similar information about themselves. Encourage students to vary or extend their answers. Circulate to give help and feedback.
6. Have several volunteers put their answers on the board. Help volunteers extend their answers if they have not already done so. Correct any errors with the whole class.
7. Have students compare their own answers with the answers on the board, then check each other's answers in pairs.

Interactions

1. & 2. GET INFORMATION/GIVE INFORMATION. *(PAGES 93 AND 94)*

Competency

[g] Follow spoken instructions about where to put things.

Step-by-Step

1. On the board or OHP, copy the first picture without the boxes of school supplies. Review prepositions of location by pointing to different places and having students say the location *(on the bottom shelf, to the right of the window)*. Write the conversation on the board or OHP without filling in the handwritten parts.
2. Review school and food vocabulary *(pens, erasers, notebooks, pencils, dictionaries, books, paper,* and *chalk; apple juice, rice, cookies, tea, tuna fish, oil,* and *peanut butter)* and write the words in two lists on the board or OHP.
3. Divide the class into a Student A group and a Student B group and have them open their books to their group's page. Show the A group that A gives information to B based on the picture, and that B must draw boxes and label them in his picture. Show the B group that the answers (the location of the boxes and their contents) come from A.
4. Fill in the conversation, read it aloud sentence by sentence, and have students repeat. Then take A's part and have a volunteer take B's part. Demonstrate that B draws a simple square to represent a box on the bottom shelf to the right of the window. Label it *books.*
5. Erase the information in the blanks and have a volunteer from each group say the conversation together for the class using *dictionaries.* Have B draw the box of dictionaries and label it. Fill in the blanks in the conversation.
6. Repeat Step 5 with two more volunteers and another cue. Have A's and B's work in pairs to fill in their pictures. Each student should change partners and do both pages. Have them compare their pictures to check their answers.

Progress Checks

1. ENDORSE THIS CHECK. *(PAGE 95)*

Competency

[f] Endorse a check or money order.

2. WHAT ARE THE PEOPLE SAYING?/ DO IT YOURSELF.

Competencies

[c] Ask to cash a check or money order.

[d] Show proper ID.

Basic Conversation

A: *Can you cash this check, please?*
B: *Do you have any identification?*
A: *Yes. Here's my driver's license.*
B: *Thank you.*

Have students use real checks and IDs or facsimilies. Encourage students to use all the cues in the conversation.

3. WHAT ARE THE PEOPLE SAYING?/ DO IT YOURSELF.

Competency

[b] Give simple excuses for lateness or absence.

Basic Conversation

A: *Where were you yesterday?*
B: *I was sick.*

Encourage students to ask questions with different past time phrases and to give different excuses.

Progress Checks

4. WHAT ARE THE PEOPLE SAYING?/ DO IT YOURSELF. *(PAGE 96)*

Competencies

[a] State a need for tools.

[e] Apologize for forgetting something.

Basic Conversation

A: *I need the hammer. Did you put it away?*
B: *Sorry. I forgot.*

Cue students with words or pictures to ask about various tools.

5. WHAT ARE THEY DOING?/ DO IT YOURSELF.

Competency

g Follow spoken instructions about where to put things.

Basic Conversation

A: *Put the dictionary on the desk. Put the pencil to the right of the dictionary.*
B: (acts out instructions)

Write simple two and three-step instructions on cards using prepositions of location. *(Take out your ID card. Put it on the floor next to your desk.)* Give the card to pairs of students who give each other instructions, and then follow them closely. Later, have students make up their own simple instructions.

Memo to the Teacher

Option

Take students to a workplace that has tools (a carpentry or drapery shop, for example). Have them take notes and/or draw a simple diagram indicating where the tools are kept. Encourage them to ask questions about the company. *(What are the hours? How often are employees paid?)* When students return to class, help them write a story together about what they saw and learned.

UNIT

9 Clothing

COMPETENCIES	GRAMMAR
Name common articles of clothing • Ask for the size you need • Respond to questions about payment • Identify incorrect change and ask for the right amount • Give simple descriptions of people • Read sizes and prices	descriptive adjectives *(tall, long, short, fat, thin, young, old, big, small)* comparative of adjectives with *-er than*

Warm-ups

1. Descriptions (Use after page 102.)
Bring magazines to class. Have students cut out pictures of three people (or more, for a greater challenge), and give them to their partners. Have them select one picture and describe it. The partner tries to identify the picture described. Then have students switch roles and continue.

2. Attributes (Use at any point in the unit.)
Arrange students in groups of four. Give each group about ten pictures of different foods, clothing, tools, and so on. Include items with different textures, colors, sizes, and numbers. Ask the groups to organize the pictures into at least two categories by color, size, number, function, and so on. Have a team member write down the categories and the items in each.

3. Twenty Questions (Use after page 99.)
Think of an object in the classroom and write it on a piece of paper. Tell the class the color and shape of the object. Have students ask up to twenty questions about it using comparatives. *(Is it bigger than a shoebox? Is it taller than the blackboard?)* Answer simply *yes* or *no*. When a student guesses the object, have her think of a new object and continue.

Getting Started

1. GUESS. *(PAGE 97)*

Establishes the context of the unit.

Step-by-Step

1. Have students look at the pictures of Gloria, her two children, and the sales clerk, and ask where they are.
2. Have students identify Gloria as one of the students, Lucy and Bonita as her children, and the man as a sales clerk.
3. Ask students to guess what Gloria and the sales clerk are saying. All responses are valid here. Respond to each guess by restating it in acceptable English.

2. WHAT CAN YOU HEAR?

Prepares students to read the first conversation on page 98.

Step-by-Step

1. Have students look at the pictures while you play the tape or read the tapescript aloud.
2. Have students volunteer any words or sentences they can recall from the conversation. Acknowledge all contributions by restating them in acceptable English.
3. Let the students hear the conversation again to elicit more of it.

Conversations

1. PRACTICE. *(PAGE 98)*

Vocabulary

clothing and sizes: *jeans, jackets, shoes, size 8*

Step-by-Step

1. Play the tape or read the conversation aloud while students follow along in their books.
2. Elicit or demonstrate the meaning of *jeans, May I help you?, over there, jackets, shoes, size,* and *Let me check.* Use the pictures on pages 97 and 98, or bring in actual articles of clothing.
3. Have students repeat the conversation sentence by sentence, and then practice in pairs.

2. WHAT CAN YOU SAY?

Vocabulary

shirt, blouse, pants, socks, sweater, skirt, dress

Step-by-Step

1. Ask students to look at the pictures and say any words they can read or guess. Use the board or OHP and write each article of clothing as it is volunteered in a place corresponding to its location on the page. After you write each item, say it, and have students point to it in their books and repeat. Add any words students have not volunteered.
2. Ask a volunteer to stand and hold up the book for the class to see. (In large classes, make smaller groups with a book held up in each.) Call on one volunteer to say an article of clothing and another to point to the picture for the class.
3. Have students work in pairs, one saying a word and the other pointing. Then have students write the articles of clothing several times, and dictate them to each other in pairs.

Option

Have students add other clothing words that they know.

NOTE: Elicit or explain that certain items of clothing are worn by women (blouses, skirts, and dresses) and others by both sexes (shirts, jeans, pants, shoes, socks, and sweaters). Men's pants sizes have the waist size first, followed by the in-seam length (32/30).

Cross-Reference

The New Oxford Picture Dictionary: Everyday Clothes, pages 20 and 21; and Underwear and Sleepwear, page 22

3. TALK ABOUT THE CLOTHES IN 2.

Competencies

a Name common articles of clothing.

b Ask for the size you need.

Step-by-Step

1. Write the conversation on the board or OHP without filling in the handwritten parts. Show students that the information for the blanks comes from Exercise 2 and fill in the blanks.
2. Read the conversation sentence by sentence, and have students repeat. Then have them repeat the items of clothing in Exercise 2.
3. Have pairs of students say the conversation for the class until all the items of clothing have been used. Then have students practice the conversation in pairs, changing partners, saying both parts, and using all the items of clothing.

NOTE: Elicit or explain that certain articles of clothing are always plural *(pants, jeans)* and take the plural verb. *(Where are my jeans?)* To count them we use *pair (a pair of jeans, two pairs of pants)*. Shoes and socks come in pairs, but can be referred to as individual items *(a shoe, two socks, a pair of shoes, two pairs of socks)*.

Cross-Reference

Multilevel Activity and Resource Package: Go Fish

Conversations

4. WHAT CAN YOU SAY? *(PAGE 99)*

Grammar

descriptive adjectives *(big, small, long, short)*

Step-by-Step

1. Ask students to look at the pictures and say any words they can read or guess. Use the board or OHP and write each word as it is volunteered in a place corresponding to its location on the page. After you write each word, say it, and have students point to it in their books and repeat. Add any words students have not volunteered and *yellow, white,* and *black.*
2. Ask a volunteer to stand and hold up the book for the class to see. (In large classes, make smaller groups with a book held up in each.) Call on one volunteer to say a word and another to point to the picture.
3. Have students work in pairs, one saying a word and the other pointing. Then have students write each word several times and dictate the words to each other in pairs.

Going Further

Have students add other colors they know and identify them using items in the room. *(Pencil—This is yellow.)*

Pronunciation

Use Minimal Pairs with *block* and *black*. (See page xi.)

Cue	Response
block	the next block
black	black shoes

Listen for the vowel sound in *block* made with the tongue low and in the back of the mouth, and the one in *black* made with the tongue far forward in the bottom of the mouth.

Cross-Reference

The New Oxford Picture Dictionary: Colors, page 104

5. PRACTICE.

Grammar

descriptive adjectives *(long, short, big, small)*
comparative of adjectives with *-er than*

Step-by-Step

1. Have students look at the picture. Encourage them to guess what Gloria and Lucy are saying.
2. Have students close their books. Play the tape or read the conversation aloud. Use stick figures to indicate which character is speaking each line.
3. Have students say anything they can recall of the conversation. Acknowledge all contributions by restating them in acceptable English.
4. Play the tape while students follow along in their books. Then elicit or demonstrate the meaning of *Mommy, How does this blouse look?, too big, Try the other blouse on, It's smaller than the yellow blouse,* and *This blouse fits.* Play the tape as many times as students need.
5. Have students repeat the conversation sentence by sentence, and practice in pairs.

Option

Expand the dialogue by acting it out with actual articles of clothing. *(How does this jacket look? It looks too small.)*

6. FOCUS ON GRAMMAR.

Grammar

descriptive adjectives *(big, small, long, short)*
comparative of adjectives with *-er than*

Step-by-Step

descriptive adjectives *(big, small)*

1. Have students look at the big and small shirts in Exercise 4. Write *The white shirt is small* and *The yellow shirt is big* in two columns on the board or OHP. Read them and have students repeat.

comparative of adjectives with *-er than* and singular nouns

2. Write *The white shirt is smaller than the yellow shirt* in a third column. Read it and have students repeat.
3. In the first column write *The black sweater is big.* Elicit a sentence for the second column with *small. (The brown sweater is small.)* Then elicit the comparative sentence for the third column. *(The black sweater is bigger than the brown sweater.)* Read the three sentences aloud and have students repeat.
4. Repeat Step 3 with *long black skirt* and *short white skirt* from Exercise 4.

comparative of adjectives with *-er than* and plural nouns

5. Have a volunteer read *The white shirts are smaller than the yellow shirts,* write it in the third column, read it, and have students repeat. Elicit the sentences for columns one and two. *(The white shirts are small* and *The yellow shirts are big.)*
6. Repeat Step 5 comparing actual garments, or refer to your own and students' clothing. Have students copy the sentences on a separate piece of paper.

7. Have a volunteer read *big, small, long,* and *short* from the first chart and write them on the board in the first column. Write *bigger* in the second column and elicit the other comparative forms. Elicit that *-er than* is used to compare two things or people. Elicit other adjectives and write their comparative forms.
8. Have students work in pairs saying and writing other sentences. Have volunteers write their sentences on the board, correct them with the whole class, and have students read them.

7. TALK ABOUT THE CLOTHES.

Grammar

descriptive adjectives *(short, long, small, big)*
comparative of adjectives with *-er than*

Step-by-Step

1. Write the conversation on the board or OHP without filling in the handwritten parts. Have students identify the size, color, and kind of clothing depicted in the pictures. Write them on the board if necessary. Show students that the information for the blanks comes from the pictures. Fill in the blanks.
2. Read the conversation aloud and have students repeat. Have pairs of students say the conversation for the class until both pictures have been described.
3. Have students practice in pairs, changing partners, saying both parts, and using all the pictures.

Cross-Reference

Multilevel Activity and Resource Package: Picture Story

Going Further

Use Word Cards from the *Multilevel Activity and Resource Package.* Have students unscramble sentences with *this/these* and articles of clothing *(this sweater/blouse/jacket* and *these pants/jeans/shoes).*

Conversations

8. WHAT CAN YOU SAY? *(PAGE 100)*

Vocabulary

cash, charge, receipt

Step-by-Step

1. Ask students to look at the pictures and say any words they can read or guess. Use the board or OHP and write each word as it is volunteered in a place corresponding to its location on the page. After you write each word, say it, and have students point to it in their books and repeat. Add any words students have not volunteered.
2. Ask a volunteer to stand and hold up the book for the class to see. (In large classes, make smaller groups with a book held up in each.) Call on a volunteer to say a word and another to point to the picture.
3. Have students work in pairs, one saying a word and another pointing. Then have them write each word several times and dictate to each other in pairs.

9. PRACTICE.

Competency

c Respond to questions about payment.

d Identify incorrect change and ask for the right amount.

Step-by-Step

1. Have students look at the picture. Encourage them to guess what Gloria and the cashier are saying.
2. Have students close their books. Play the tape or read the conversation aloud, indicating who is speaking each line.
3. Have students say anything they can recall of the conversation. Acknowledge all contributions by restating them in acceptable English.
4. Play the tape while students follow along in their books. Then elicit or demonstrate the meaning *That comes to…, Here you are, Here's your change,* and *My change should be….* Play the tape as many times as students need.
5. Have students repeat the conversation sentence by sentence and practice in pairs.

NOTE: Teach *My change should be…* as a formula rather than introducing *should* as a modal auxiliary.

Explain the difference between *cash* and *charge* by bringing in an actual credit card and some bills and coins. Elicit or explain that a credit card charges interest. Also elicit how much the *sales tax* is for your state.

10. TALK ABOUT A PURCHASE. B, FIGURE OUT THE CHANGE.

Competencies

c Respond to questions about payment.

d Identify incorrect change and ask for the right amount.

Step-by-Step

1. Write the conversation on the board or OHP without filling in the handwritten parts. Show students that the information for the blanks comes from the cues below. Fill them in.

2. Read the conversation aloud sentence by sentence and have students repeat. Have them repeat the price cues. Have pairs of students say the conversation for the class until all the prices have been used.
3. Have students practice in pairs, saying both parts, and using all the prices.

Going Further

Have students make up other totals and figure out the change from a $20.00 bill.

NOTE: Telling a cashier about incorrect change is appropriate in the U.S. Tell students that cashiers must keep an accurate cash drawer or lose the money from their pay.

Cross-Reference

Multilevel Activity and Resource Package: Listening and Scrambled Sentences

Paperwork

1. READ SUE'S LIST. *(PAGE 101)*

Reading sizes and prices.

Step-by-Step

1. Draw an outline of the list on the board or OHP.
2. Have volunteers say any words or phrases from the list they can read or guess. As each word is said, write it on the board, say it, and have students repeat.
3. Elicit or supply missing items in the same way.
4. Elicit or demonstrate the meaning of words on the form by asking questions about it. *(What is Sue's dress size? Whose jacket is smaller than Sue's?)*
5. Point to items in the completed list at random and have students read them aloud. Leave the list on the board.

Going Further

Have students add other clothing to the list. Have them assign a size to each new article of clothing based on what they know about the Lee family.

NOTE: Children's clothes are sized by their age. Women's clothing sizes are even numbers; junior girls' sizes are odd numbers.

2. THESE ARE THE LEE FAMILY'S NEW CLOTHES. WRITE THEIR NAMES NEXT TO THEIR CLOTHES.

Identifying clothing sizes and matching the owners with their clothes.

Step-by-Step

1. Hold up the book and point to the dress. Elicit *dress* and *size 8.* Draw an outline of the dress with a size 8 tag on the board or OHP. Point to the list in Exercise 1, find the dress column, point to *size 8,* and identify Minh as the person who wears that size. Write *Minh* next to the dress on the board.
2. Have students identify the owners of the clothing by writing the names in their books. When they finish, have them check their answers with another student.
3. Have volunteers draw outlines of the clothing on the board. Have other volunteers write the owners' names on the board. Have the class correct any errors.

3. INTERVIEW THREE CLASSMATES.

Gives practice speaking and writing.

Step-by-Step

1. Copy the questions on the board or OHP, not filling in Sue's information yet.
2. Invite a student to speak for Sue. Interview "Sue" and answer the questions with students' help.
3. Say the interview questions one at a time and have students repeat them.
4. Have a volunteer interview you and write your answers on the board. Correct the answers with the whole class.
5. Have students ask and answer the questions with three classmates and write the answers on a separate piece of paper.

Reading and Writing

1. WHAT CAN YOU SAY ABOUT BONITA? USE THESE WORDS. *(PAGE 102)*

Pre-reading.

Step-by-Step

1. Have students look at the six captioned pictures and say or read anything they can. As each word is suggested, write it on the board or OHP, say it, and have students repeat.
2. Have students look at Bonita's picture. Ask questions *(How old do you think Bonita is? How tall is she? What is she wearing?).*

Going Further

Have a student leave the room. Have the class describe her from memory, including physical features and clothing. Write their words, phrases, or sentences on the board or OHP. Have the student return to the classroom and compare the description with the facts.

NOTE: Students need to know that age and weight are sensitive topics in U.S. culture. Therefore, instead of hurting feelings by saying *She's old and fat,* tell students more diplomatic terms. *(She's in her eighties and a little overweight.)*

2. READ GLORIA'S DESCRIPTION OF BONITA.

Reading stories.

Step-by-Step

1. Give students time to look at the story and read what they can. Play the tape or read the story while students follow in their books.
2. Play the tape one sentence at a time and have students repeat. Then have volunteers read sentences of the story aloud.

Going Further

Have students rewrite the story about twin girls. Start with *My daughters' names are Eva and Maria.*

Going Still Further

Have students compute Bonita's height and weight in centimeters and kilos. Have them convert their own weight from the metric system into feet, inches, and pounds.

3. FILL IN THE MISSING PERSON FORM FOR BONITA.

Comprehension check.

Step-by-Step

1. Write the form on the board without filling in the handwritten parts. Elicit *Bonita Rivas* for the first blank by asking *What is her name?* Fill in the blank. Elicit *a yellow shirt* for the clothing blank by asking *What is she wearing?*
2. Pair students to complete the exercise. Send volunteers to the board to write their answers.
3. Correct the answers with the whole class. Leave the form on the board for Exercise 5.

Cross-Reference

Multilevel Activity and Resource Package: Grammar and Game: Who Is It?

Reading and Writing

4. WHAT CAN YOU SAY? *(PAGE 103)*

Vocabulary

striped, polka-dotted, print, plaid, checked

Step-by-Step

1. Ask students to look at the pictures and say any words they can. Use the board or OHP and write each word as it is volunteered in a place corresponding to its location on the page. After you write each word, say it, and have students point to it in their books and repeat. Add any words students have not volunteered.
2. Ask a volunteer to stand and hold up the book for the class to see. (In large classes, make smaller groups with a book held up in each.) Call on one volunteer to say a word and another to point to the picture for the class.
3. Have students work in pairs, one saying a word and the other pointing. Then have students write the words several times, and dictate them to each other in pairs.

Cross-Reference

The New Oxford Picture Dictionary: Describing Clothes, page 24

Option

Bring in actual clothing with different patterns for hands-on practice.

5. FILL IN THE MISSING PERSON FORM.

Filling in a form.

Step-by-Step

1. Bring in pictures illustrating various hair and eye colors. Ask volunteers to describe the pictures. List the hair and eye colors on the board.
2. Go back to the form on the board from Exercise 3 and erase the information. Point to one of the people in Exercise 4 and ask students questions about him or her to elicit information for the first two blanks. *(What is his name? How old is she?)* Write the answers on the board.
3. Have students choose one of the people in Exercise 4, and use their imagination to fill in the blanks.
4. Pair students to check their work.

Option

Have students write a second missing person form for a different person in Exercise 4.

6. WRITE A DESCRIPTION OF THE PERSON.

Competency

e Give simple descriptions of people.

Step-by-Step

1. Tell the class about one of the people in Exercise 4, using Bonita's description in Exercise 2 as a model. Help students restate what you have said to confirm their understanding. Then write the paragraph on the board or OHP. Leave your description on the board for students to use as a model.
2. Have students write their descriptions on a separate piece of paper. Encourage them to help each other. Circulate to give help as needed or to listen to students' descriptions.
3. Have students work in pairs reading their descriptions and having their partners restate to confirm understanding.

7. READ YOUR DESCRIPTION TO YOUR GROUP. GROUP, POINT TO THE PERSON IN 4.

Lets students share their writing and check comprehension.

Step-by-Step

1. Have a volunteer read her description aloud to the class. Lead the class in applause for the reader.
2. Have the class restate the description to confirm understanding. Encourage the volunteer to clarify meaning, if necessary. Have students point to the person being described in Exercise 4.
3. Have students work in groups of four to read their descriptions in turn and to receive applause and responses from their peers. Then publish the descriptions by posting them in the classroom.

Cross-Reference

Multilevel Activity and Resource Package: Jigsaw Reading and Concentration

Listening Plus

1. WHAT'S NEXT? *(PAGE 104)*

Predicting with social and grammatical clues.

Step-by-Step

1. Have students close their books. Write the first response for *a* on the board or OHP. Read it aloud and have students repeat.
2. Have students work in pairs to guess what might come before.
3. Have pairs volunteer their ideas. Help the class evaluate each one.
4. Do the same with the other responses in *a.* Leave the responses on the board.
5. Have students open their books and have a volunteer come to the board.
6. Play the tape or read the tapescript aloud one conversation at a time. Have students point to the correct response in their books and have the volunteer point to it at the board. Play the tape as many times as students need.
7. Repeat the process for *b.*

2. REVIEW...WRITE... NUMBER.

Focused listening.

ANSWER KEY

Write: b. *$14.00;* c. *$40.00;* d. *$39.95;* e. *$30.95;* f. *$139.95*

Number: a. *1;* b. *5;* c. *3;* d. *4;* e. *2;* f. *6*

REVIEW.

Step-by-Step

1. Have students look at the clothing and say anything they can about it. Acknowledge all contributions by restating them in acceptable English.
2. As vocabulary from the unit is volunteered, write it on the board or OHP, say it, and have students repeat.
3. Elicit any other vocabulary which will be helpful in distinguishing among the items.
4. Point to items on the board at random and have volunteers read them aloud.

WRITE.

Step-by-Step

1. Copy the picture of the items with their price tags on the board or OHP.
2. Play the tape or read the first conversation aloud. Fill in the first price *($44.00)* as students hear it.
3. Continue playing the tape one conversation at a time and have students fill in the other prices. Play the tape as many times as students need.
4. Have students compare their answers in pairs.
5. Play the tape again, one conversation at a time. Have a volunteer write the answers on the board. Correct the student's answers with the whole class.
6. Have students check their answers against the answers on the board, then play the tape once more so that students can verify their answers.

NUMBER.

Step-by-Step

1. Play the tape or read the tapescript aloud one conversation at a time, as many times as students need. Have students number the clothing in the order of the conversations they hear.
2. Have students compare their answers in pairs.
3. Play the tape again and have a volunteer write the answers on the board. Correct any errors with the whole class.
4. Have students check their answers against the answers on the board, then play the tape once more so that students can verify their answers.

3. A, DESCRIBE THE CLOTHES IN 2. B, SAY WHAT YOU HEARD AND POINT.

Speaking and active listening.

Step-by-Step

1. Have volunteers make statements about one of the items of clothing in Exercise 2. Repeat each statement. Demonstrate the use of clarification strategies (for example, *How much?, What size?,* or *What color?).*
2. Have students hold up their books and point to the item of clothing described.
3. Have students work in pairs to make statements, restate, and point. Each student should change partners and describe all the clothing. Circulate to listen and give help as needed.

4. WHAT ABOUT YOU?

Listening and responding with personal information.

Step-by-Step

1. Play the tape once. Have students confer in groups to reconstruct the statement they heard. Circulate to hear what they say.
2. Repeat Step 1 until most groups have the gist of the statement.
3. Have groups share their reconstructions and help them reach a consensus.
4. Play the tape again so that students can verify their reconstruction.
5. Have students answer the question on the tape by writing similar information about themselves. Encourage students to vary or extend their answers. Circulate to give help and feedback.
6. Have several volunteers put their answers on the board. Help volunteers extend their answers if they have not already done so. Correct any errors with the whole class.
7. Have students compare their own answers with the answers on the board, then check each other's answers in pairs.

Cross-Reference

Multilevel Activity and Resource Package: Game: Win, Lose, or Draw

Interactions

1. & 2. GET INFORMATION/GIVE INFORMATION. *(PAGES 105 AND 106)*

Competency

[f] Read sizes and prices.

Step-by-Step

1. Review the vocabulary for sizes, colors, and clothing in this exercise, if necessary, by having students describe clothing they or other students are wearing. *(Geraldo's wearing a plaid shirt. I'm wearing a red jacket.)* On the board or OHP, write the conversation without filling in the handwritten parts, and write the first four items on A's shopping list *(grey pants, size 32/32; black pants, size 32/36; white sweater, size S/ yellow sweater, size M)*.
2. Divide the class into a Student A group and a Student B group, and have them open their books to their group's page. Have the A group point to the blanks on their list and the B group point to the pictures. Then have students switch roles for part 2.
3. Fill in the conversation, read it aloud sentence by sentence, and have students repeat.
4. Take A's part and have an able student take B's part. Fill in the first two shopping list blanks. Have volunteers from both groups say the conversation. Erase the information in the blanks. Call on new volunteers to say the conversation using *white sweater, size small* and *yellow sweater, size medium.* Fill in the blanks in the conversation and shopping list.
5. Have students work in pairs to fill in the information. Each student should change roles and partners and do both pages. Have students add up the prices and write the total cost at the bottom of the shopping list. Have students compare their answers.

Going Further

Have students add more items to the shopping lists and continue.

Cross-Reference

Multilevel Activity and Resource Package: Categories, Writing, and Sorting

Progress Checks

1. FILL IN THE PRICES. *(PAGE 107)*

Competency

[f] Read sizes and prices.

2. WHAT ARE THE PEOPLE SAYING?/ DO IT YOURSELF.

Competencies

[a] Name common articles of clothing.

[b] Ask for the size you need.

Basic Conversation

A: *Do you have this sweater in small?*
B: *Let me check.*

For *Do It Yourself,* use pictures or word cards to cue students to ask about many different types of clothing and sizes.

Progress Checks

3. WHAT ARE THE PEOPLE SAYING?/ DO IT YOURSELF. *(PAGE 108)*

Competency

[e] Give simple descriptions of people.

Basic Conversation

A: *He isn't tall and he isn't short. He has blond hair and brown eyes. He's wearing a jacket.*
B: *It's Boris!*

For *Do It Yourself,* have students work in pairs. One student describes someone else to the other; the other student guesses names. The first student repeats or expands her description until the person is identified.

4. WHAT ARE THE PEOPLE SAYING?/ DO IT YOURSELF.

Competencies

c Respond to questions about payment.

d Identify incorrect change and ask for the right amount.

Basic Conversation

A: *That comes to $22.00. Is that cash or charge?*
B: *Cash.*
A: *Thank you. Here's your change.*
B: *Excuse me. I gave you $40.00. My change should be $18.00.*
A: *I'm sorry. Here you are.*
B: *That's OK. No problem.*

For *Do It Yourself,* to demonstrate competency, students need to show that they know when change is wrong, and that they can calculate the correct change. Bring in register tapes and play money. Coach "cashiers" to give the *right* change sometimes.

Memo to the Teacher

Have students write their own shopping lists and check them in pairs. Then take the class to your local J Mart-type store, or have them go on their own to different stores. Have them fill in the prices on their lists or write *no* if the item isn't available. Then, in class, have them compare prices for similar items.

UNIT 10 Transportation

COMPETENCIES	GRAMMAR
Ask and answer questions about departure and arrival times • Read departure and arrival schedules • Buy travel tickets, asking about fares • Read common traffic and pedestrian signs • Give information about the trip from your home country to the United States	*ever, always, usually, sometimes, hardly ever, never*

Warm-ups

BEFORE  CLASS

1. Islamabad (Use at any point in the unit.)
Describe a place (your home town, house or room) that is special to you in a few sentences. As you describe it, use Cuisenaire rods or other small objects to show what you are saying. Then ask volunteers to restate what you have said, pointing to the rods as they speak. Then have students work in pairs with the rods to describe places and restate.

BEFORE  CLASS

2. Collage (Use at any point in the unit.)
Have students cut out pictures from magazines that reflect different emotions. Have students select a picture that illustrates their feelings for today, state how they feel, and give reasons, if they wish. Provide a poster board and glue for students to create a picture collage.

3. Visualization (Use after page 110.)
Have students imagine that they are going to take a wonderful trip for free. Ask questions. *(Where are you going to go? How are you going to travel there? How long are you going to stay?)* Give students time to think and then share their fantasies in small groups. After each description, have others restate to confirm understanding.

Getting Started

1. GUESS. *(PAGE 109)*

Establishes the context of the unit.

Step-by-Step

1. Have students look at the picture of Donna and Young Ho and ask where they are.
2. Have students identify Donna as the teacher and Young Ho as one of her students. Ask students to guess what Donna and Young Ho are saying. All responses are valid here. Respond to each guess by restating it in acceptable English.

2. WHAT CAN YOU HEAR?

Prepares students to read the first conversation on page 110.

1. Have students look at the picture while you play the tape or read the tapescript aloud.
2. Have students volunteer any words or sentences they can recall from the conversation. Acknowledge all contributions by restating them in acceptable English.
3. Let students hear the conversation again to elicit more of it.

Conversations

1. PRACTICE. *(PAGE 110)*

Grammar

always, usually, sometimes, hardly ever, never

Step-by-Step

1. Play the tape or read the conversation aloud while students follow along in their books.
2. Elicit or demonstrate the meaning of *That's nice, take the train/bus,* and *How long is the trip?* by using the picture on page 109 and of *never, hardly ever,* and *usually,* by drawing a time line:

0%	/	50%	/	100%
never	hardly ever	sometimes	usually	always

3. Have students repeat the conversation sentence by sentence and then practice in pairs.

Pronunciation

Use Minimal Pairs with *bus* and *boss.* (See page xi.) *Bus* has the same vowel sound as in *come* and *but.* The vowel for *boss* is made with the tongue lower in the mouth and pulled toward the back, with the lips slightly rounded.

Cue	**Response**
bus	Take the bus.
boss	Mr. Ross is the boss.

Cross-Reference

The New Oxford Picture Dictionary: Public Transportation, pages 54 and 55

2. FOCUS ON GRAMMAR.

Grammar

always, usually, sometimes, hardly ever, never

Step-by-Step

***ever* in present tense questions; *always, usually, sometimes, hardly ever, never* in *yes/no* short answers**

1. Write the first question on the board or OHP and have students repeat. Elicit as many questions as students can produce beginning with *Do you ever,* write them under the first question, and have students repeat each one.
2. Put the time line from Exercise 1 on the board again.
3. Have students ask each other the questions and answer with adverbs from the time line. After each answer, repeat it with *Yes* or *No*, as appropriate, and have students repeat. Encourage truthful answers.
4. Continue with other questions and answers until you believe students are aware which adverbs take *yes* and which take *no.*
5. Have volunteers circle the two sets on the time line and write out the short answers on the board to verify their understanding.
6. Have students generate other questions and answers orally and in writing. Have some students put their work on the board, correct them with the whole class, and have students copy them.

***always, usually, sometimes, hardly ever, never* in statements with *be* and other verbs**

7. Write the first sentence in the statement box on the board or OHP, leaving plenty of space between the words so that you can create a table. Have students repeat the sentence.
8. Write the first and last parts of a new sentence that will be meaningful to the students, leaving out the adverb and verb. Then elicit adverbs and verbs, write them on the board, and have students repeat. *(Donna and Young Ho sometimes talk after class, Young Ho's grandparents never go to Bridgeton.)*
9. To the right of this first table, write the second sentence in the box and elicit verbs and adverbs for additional sentences. *(This class is always one hour, This school is never open on Sunday.)*
10. Have students work in pairs to generate additional meaningful sentences in both patterns, orally and in writing. Have some students put their sentences on the board, correct them with the whole class, and have students copy them.

Going Further

Elicit other adverbs of frequency students know *(almost never, seldom, frequently, often, almost always)* and add them to the time line suggested for Exercise 1. Note that *seldom* falls right on the line between *yes* and *no*. Some people might say, *No, seldom,* while others might say *Yes, but seldom.*

3. WHAT CAN YOU SAY?

Vocabulary

drive to school, take the bus to work, take the train to (Chicago), fly to (your country)

Step-by-Step

1. Ask students to look at the pictures and say any words they can read or guess. Use the board or OHP and write each mode of transportation as it is volunteered in a place corresponding to its location on the page. After you write each phrase, say it, and have students point to it in their books and repeat. Add any words students have not volunteered.
2. Ask a volunteer to stand and hold up the book for the class to see. (In large classes, make

smaller groups with a book held up in each.) Call on one volunteer to say a mode of transportation and another to point to the picture for the class.

3. Have students work in pairs, one saying a phrase and the other pointing. Then have students write the modes of transportation several times, and dictate them to each other in pairs.

Option

Have students add other modes of transportation they know: *walking, ride a bike/motorcycle, take a boat/ship, skate,* etc.

4. TALK ABOUT YOURSELF.

Grammar

ever, always, usually, sometimes, hardly ever, never

Step-by-Step

1. Write the conversation on the board or OHP without filling in the handwritten parts. Show students that the information for the blanks comes from Exercise 3. Fill in the blanks.
2. Read the conversation aloud and have students repeat. Show students that the answer can be *Yes, sometimes (always, usually)* or *No, never (hardly ever)*. Have them repeat the modes of transportation in Exercise 3 and the adverbs of frequency in Exercise 2. Have a volunteer say the conversation with you. Then erase the information in the blanks.
3. Replace the blanks with new information. Have two volunteers say the conversation for the class. Then have pairs of students say the conversation for the class until all the modes of transportation in Exercise 3 and all the adverbs in Exercise 2 have been used.
4. Have students practice in pairs, changing partners, saying both parts, and using all the modes of transportation and adverbs.

Going Further

Include the other modes of transportation added in Exercise 3.

Cross-Reference

Multilevel Activity and Resource Package: Word Tap

Conversations

5. PRACTICE. *(PAGE 111)*

Competency

[a] Ask and answer questions about departure and arrival times.

Step-by-Step

1. Have students look at the picture of Young Ho and the ticket agent. Encourage them to guess what they are saying.
2. Have students close their books. Play the tape or read the conversation aloud, indicating who is speaking each line.
3. Have students say anything they can recall of the conversation. Acknowledge all contributions by restating them in acceptable English. If necessary, practice saying the time *9:45 a.m., 1:37 p.m., 12:45 p.m.*, and *4:50 p.m.*
4. Play the tape while students follow along in their books. Then elicit the meaning of *get there* and *the Los Angeles bus* (the bus going to Los Angeles).
5. Have students repeat the conversation sentence by sentence and practice in pairs.

6. WHAT CAN YOU SAY?

Vocabulary

map locations: U.S. cities and states

Step-by-Step

1. Ask students to look at the picture and say any cities they know or can read. Use the board or OHP. Draw an outline of the U.S. and write each city as it is volunteered. After you write each city, say it, and have students point to it in their books and repeat. Add any cities students have not volunteered.
2. Ask two volunteers to come to the board. Have one volunteer say a city, and the other point to it on the map.
3. Have students work in pairs, one saying a city and the other pointing. Then have them write each city and dictate the names to each other.

Going Further

Have students add their own cities and nearby towns to the map.

7. TALK ABOUT THE BUS SCHEDULES.

Competency

[a] Ask and answer questions about departure and arrival times.

[b] Read departure and arrival schedules.

Step-by-Step

1. Write the conversation on the board or OHP without filling in the handwritten parts. Show students that the information comes from the bus schedule. Fill in the blanks.
2. Read the conversation aloud and have students repeat. Also have them repeat the information in the bus schedule. Have pairs of students say the conversation for the class until all the times and destinations have been used.
3. Have students practice in pairs, changing partners, saying both parts, and using all the times and destinations.

Cross-Reference

Multilevel Activity and Resource Package: Grammar

Conversations

8. WHAT CAN YOU SAY? *(PAGE 112)*

Vocabulary

one-way, round-trip

Step-by-Step

1. Ask students to look at the pictures and say any words they can read or guess. Use the board or OHP and write each word as it is volunteered in a place corresponding to its location on the page. After you write each word, say it, and have students point to it in their books and repeat. Add any words students have not volunteered.
2. Ask a volunteer to stand and hold up the book for the class to see. (In large classes, make smaller groups with a book held up in each.) Call on a volunteer to say a word and another to point to the picture.
3. Have students work in pairs, one saying a word and the other pointing. Then have them write each word several times and dictate them to each other in pairs.

9. PRACTICE.

Competency

[c] Buy travel tickets, asking about fares.

Step-by-Step

1. Have students guess what Young Ho and the ticket agent are saying now.
2. Have students close their books. Play the tape or read the conversation aloud and indicate who is speaking each line.
3. Have students say anything they can recall of the conversation. Acknowledge all contributions by restating them in acceptable English.
4. Play the tape while students follow along in their books. Then elicit or demonstrate the meaning of *Here you are, Here's your ticket,* and *L.A.* Play the tape as many times as students need.
5. Have students repeat the conversation sentence by sentence and practice in pairs.

10. TALK ABOUT ONE-WAY AND ROUND-TRIP TICKETS.

Competency

[c] Buy travel tickets, asking about fares.

Step-by-Step

1. Write the conversation on the board or OHP. Show students that the information from the blanks comes from the fare schedule below and fill it in.
2. Read the conversation sentence by sentence and have students repeat. Also have them repeat the fares. Show students they can choose to buy a *one-way* or a *round-trip* ticket to the same city.
3. Have pairs of students say the conversation for the class until all the fares have been used. Then have students practice the conversation in pairs, changing partners, saying both parts, and using all the fares.

Going Further

Have students add the ticket class *(first class, economy, coach,* or *super-saver).*

Cross-Reference

Multilevel Activity and Resource Package: Picture Story, Listening, and Scrambled Sentences

Paperwork

1. SUMI SEES THESE SIGNS ON HER WAY TO SCHOOL. READ THE SIGNS. *(PAGE 113)*

Reading traffic signs.

Step-by-Step

1. Draw outlines of the traffic signs on the board or OHP.
2. Have volunteers say any words or phrases from the signs in the book they can read or guess. As each item is suggested, draw the symbol, write its name, say it aloud, and have students repeat.
3. Elicit or supply missing items in the same way.
4. Elicit or demonstrate the meaning of *pedestrian crossing, disabled parking, walk (across the crosswalk), railroad crossing, school crossing,* and *don't walk.*
5. Point to signs at random and have students read them aloud.

Going Further

Have students add other signs they know *(bus stop, yield, stop, no parking,* or *one way).*

2. WRITE THE NUMBER OF THE SIGN IN 1.

Competency

[d] Read common traffic and pedestrian signs.

Step-by-Step

1. Write *Disabled Parking Only* on the board or OHP. Have students look at the signs in Exercise 1 and find the number of the appropriate sign. Fill in the blank. Read the list of signs in Exercise 2 and have students repeat.
2. Have students complete the exercise and check their answers with a partner.
3. Write the remaining list of signs on the board and have volunteers fill in their answers. Have students check their work and correct their answers.

3. INTERVIEW THREE CLASSMATES.

Speaking and writing.

Step-by-Step

1. Write the interview questions on the board or OHP, without filling in Sumi's information.
2. Invite a student to speak for Sumi. Interview "Sumi" and write her answers with students' help.
3. Say the interview questions one at a time and have students repeat them.
4. Have a volunteer interview you and write your answers on the board. Correct the answers with the whole class.
5. Have students ask and answer the questions with three classmates and write their answers on a separate piece of paper.

Going Further

Have students draw simple versions of local signs which differ from those in the book.

Going Still Further

Have students ask additional questions. *(What other signs can you see on your way to school? How do you usually get to school?)*

Cross-Reference

Multilevel Activity and Resource Package: Concentration

Reading and Writing

1. WHAT CAN YOU SAY ABOUT PABLO'S TRIP TO THE UNITED STATES? *(PAGE 114)*

Pre-reading.

Step-by-Step

1. Have students look at the pictures of Pablo's trip to the United States and say any words or sentences they can. As each word, phrase, or sentence is suggested, write it on the board or OHP, say it, and have students repeat.
2. Add any key phrases from the reading that students have not volunteered, including *village* and *visa.* Point to items at random and have students read them aloud.

2. READ PABLO'S STORY.

Reading stories.

Step-by-Step

1. Give students time to look at the story and read what they can. Play the tape or read the story while students follow in their books.
2. Play the tape one sentence at a time and have students repeat. Then have volunteers read sentences of the story aloud.

3. CIRCLE THE ANSWER THAT COMPLETES THE SENTENCE CORRECTLY.

Comprehension check.

Step-by-Step

1. Write *a. Pablo is from a village Los Angeles Mexico City* on the board or OHP. Read it aloud and have students repeat. Elicit the answer *(a village)* and circle it.
2. Pair students to finish the exercise. While they are working, write all the sentences on the board. Have volunteers circle their answers on the board and read the completed sentences aloud.

Option

Have students rewrite the sentences in paragraph form and change *Pablo* to *Pablo and Maria,* and make the appropriate changes.

Cross-Reference

Multilevel Activity and Resource Package: Sequencing

Reading and Writing

4. DRAW LINES. *(Page 115)*

Competency

[e] Give information about the trip from your home country to the United States.

Step-by-Step

1. Draw a simple outline map of Mexico and the United States on the board or OHP. Have volunteers help locate Pablo's village on the map, Mexico City, Los Angeles, and Bridgeton. Mark each place with a dot and label it.
2. Have a volunteer draw a line connecting these places. As each part of the trip is drawn, have volunteers say sentences describing that leg of Pablo's trip. *(Pablo went from his village to the bus station by truck. He went to Mexico City by bus.)*
3. Have students trace their route to the United States from their home country by drawing lines on the map in their books.
4. Pair students. Have each partner trace his route with his finger and describe each leg of his trip. Have his partner repeat the story to confirm understanding, and then switch roles.

Option

In Step 1, use a large wall map, string, and tacks to trace Pablo's route. After Step 4, have students use tacks and string to show their own trips to the U.S.

5. ANSWER THESE QUESTIONS ABOUT YOURSELF.

Competency

[e] Give information about the trip from your home country to the United States.

Step-by-Step

1. Read each question aloud and have students repeat.
2. Have different volunteers read the questions and have one volunteer answer. Write his answers on the board and correct them. If necessary, model one answer as a guide for the volunteer. Teach *I came here alone.* Then let students practice in pairs.
3. Have students write their answers on a separate piece of paper. Encourage students to help each other. Circulate to give help as needed.

NOTE: Acknowledging students' conflicting and changing feelings about leaving home and living in the United States can be helpful to them.

6. WRITE A STORY ABOUT YOURSELF.

Multi-sentence writing.

Step-by-Step

1. Tell your own story one paragraph at a time, using Pablo's story as a model. After each paragraph, help students restate what you have said to confirm their understanding. Then write the paragraph on the board or OHP. Leave your story on the board for students to use as a model.
2. Have students work in pairs, telling their stories to each other. Have partners restate the story to confirm understanding. Then have them switch roles.
3. Have students write their stories. Encourage them to help each other. Circulate to give help as needed or to listen to students' stories.

Option

For Step 1, use the volunteer's answers from Exercise 5 as a basis for the model story. Rewrite the sentences in paragraph form.

Cross-Reference

Multilevel Activity and Resource Package:
Writing and Categories

7. READ YOUR STORY TO YOUR GROUP.

Lets students share their writing.

Step-by-Step

1. Have a volunteer read his story aloud to the class. Then lead the class in applause.
2. Help the class restate the story to confirm understanding, and help the volunteer clarify meaning, if necessary.
3. Have students work in groups of four to read their own stories, confirm understanding of their classmates' stories, and applaud them.
4. Have students copy their stories on a separate piece of paper. Then publish the stories by posting them in the classroom.

Listening Plus

1. WHAT'S NEXT? *(PAGE 116)*

Predicting with social and grammatical clues.

Step-by-Step

1. Have students close their books. Write the first response for *a* on the board or OHP. Read it aloud and have students repeat.
2. Have students work in pairs to guess what might come before.
3. Have pairs volunteer their ideas. Help the class evaluate each one.
4. Do the same with the other responses in *a*. Leave the responses on the board.
5. Have students open their books and have a volunteer come to the board.
6. Play the tape or read the tapescript aloud one conversation at a time. Have students point to the correct response in their books and have the volunteer point to it at the board. Play the tape as many times as students need.
7. Repeat the process for *b*.

2. REVIEW...WRITE...NUMBER.

Focused listening.

ANSWER KEY

Write: a. *departure 7:30 a.m., arrival 9:55 p.m.;* b. *departure 6:00 a.m., arrival 11:55 a.m.;* c. *departure 7:30 a.m., arrival 9:55 a.m.;* d. *departure 6:00 p.m., arrival 11:55 p.m.;* e. *departure 7:00 a.m., arrival 8:30 a.m.;* f. *departure 7 p.m., arrival 8:30 p.m.*

Number: a. *5;* b. *1;* c. *2;* d. *3;* e. *4;* f. *6*

REVIEW.

Step-by-Step

1. Have students look at the notes and read or say anything they can about them. Acknowledge all contributions by restating them in acceptable English.
2. As vocabulary from the unit is volunteered, write it on the board or OHP, say it, and have students repeat.
3. Elicit any other vocabulary which will be helpful in distinguishing among the items.
4. Point to items on the board at random and have volunteers read them aloud.

WRITE.

Step-by-Step

1. Copy the answer blanks on the board or OHP.
2. Play the tape or read the first conversation aloud. Fill in the first departure and arrival time as students hear it.
3. Continue playing the tape one conversation at a time and have students fill in the other answers. Play the tape as many times as students need.
4. Have students compare their answers in pairs.
5. Play the tape again, one conversation at a time. Have a volunteer write the answers on the board. Correct the student's answers with the whole class.
6. Have students check their answers against the answers on the board, then play the tape once more so that students can verify their answers.

NUMBER.

Step-by-Step

1. Play the tape or read the tapescript aloud one conversation at a time, as many times as students need. Have students number the notes in the order of the conversations they hear.
2. Have students compare their answers in pairs.
3. Play the tape again and have a volunteer write the answers on the board. Correct any errors with the whole class.
4. Have students check their answers against the answers on the board, then play the tape once more so that students can verify their answers.

3. A, TELL WHERE YOU WANT TO GO AND HOW YOU WANT TO TRAVEL. B, SAY WHAT YOU HEARD AND POINT.

Speaking and active listening.

Step-by-Step

1. Have volunteers make statements about one of the trips in Exercise 2. Repeat each statement. Demonstrate the use of clarification strategies (for example, *When?*, *Where?*, or *How?*).
2. Have students hold up their books and point to the trip described.
3. Have students work in pairs to make statements, restate, and point. Each student should change partners and describe all the trips. Circulate to listen and give help as needed.

4. WHAT ABOUT YOU?

Listening and responding with personal information.

Step-by-Step

1. Play the tape once. Have students confer in groups to reconstruct the statement they heard. Circulate to hear what they say.
2. Repeat Step 1 until most groups have the gist of the statement.
3. Have groups share their reconstructions and help them reach a consensus.
4. Play the tape again so that students can verify their reconstruction.
5. Have students answer the question on the tape by writing similar information about themselves. Encourage students to vary or extend their answers. Circulate to give help and feedback.
6. Have several volunteers put their answers on the board. Help volunteers extend their answers if they have not already done so. Correct any errors with the whole class.
7. Have students compare their own answers with the answers on the board, then check each other's answers in pairs.

Interactions

1. & 2. GIVE INFORMATION/GET INFORMATION. *(PAGES 117 AND 118)*

Information gap for communicative practice.

Step-by-Step

1. Write the conversation on the board or OHP. Review the spelling of the names of cities and countries by pairing students and having Student A ask B to spell the name of his home town and country. After B spells them, they switch roles.
2. Divide the class into a Student A group and Student B group, and ask them to open their books to their group's page. Have the A group point to their filled-in maps and the B group point to the missing information on their maps. Then have students switch roles for Olga's trip, Exercise 2.
3. Read the conversation aloud sentence by sentence and have students repeat. Have volunteers from both groups say the conversation. Erase it from the board. Call on new

volunteers to continue the conversation using the first city *(Saigon)*. (B: *What city is he from?* A: *He's from Saigon.* B: *How do you spell Saigon?* A: *S-A-I-G-O-N.)* Show students how to fill in the information on the map.

4. Have students work in pairs to do the exercises. Each student should change partners and do both pages.

Cross-Reference

Multilevel Activity and Resource Package: Jigsaw Reading and Game: Going Home

Progress Checks

1. MATCH *(PAGE 119)*

Competency

[d] Read common traffic and pedestrian signs.

2. WHAT ARE THE PEOPLE SAYING?/ DO IT YOURSELF.

Competencies

[a] Ask and answer questions about departure and arrival times.

[b] Read departure and arrival schedules.

Basic Conversation

A: *What times does the Denver plane leave, please?*
B: *11:00 a.m.*
A: *And what time does it get there?*
B: *1:00 p.m.*

In *Do It Yourself,* encourage students to add other cities and departure/arrival times to the schedule.

Progress Checks

3. WHAT ARE THE PEOPLE SAYING?/ DO IT YOURSELF. *(PAGE 120)*

Competency

[c] Buy travel tickets, asking about fares.

Basic Conversation

A: *I'd like a ticket to Denver, please.*
B: *One-way or round-trip?*
A: *One-way. How much is it?*
B: *$149.00.*

In *Do It Yourself,* have students work in pairs, using different destinations, types of tickets, and amounts. Encourage them to use clarification strategies if needed.

4. WHAT ARE THE PEOPLE SAYING?/ DO IT YOURSELF.

Competency

[e] Give information about the trip from your home country to the United States.

Basic Conversation

A: *When did you come to the United States?*
B: *In 1987.*
A: *How did you get here?*
B: *I took the bus to Lima. Then I flew to Los Angeles.*

In *Do It Yourself,* to demonstrate competency, students should tell their own stories in as much detail as they can manage.

Memo to the Teacher

Option

Have groups of students plan a ten day vacation trip together. They must agree on a destination; decide on their means of transportation; figure out the cost of transportation by calling railroads, airlines, or bus lines, or by estimating the cost of driving; figure out the time they will spend traveling; and figure out how many nights they will need to stay in a hotel. In their reports to the class, have them use a map to show their route, and explain why they decided on this travel plan.

Crossroads 2, Unit 1: Introductions

Group Competency Checklist

Teacher ____________________

Class ____________________

NAMES	a Introduce yourself.	b Introduce others.	c Say where you are from.	d Say *Goodbye*.	e Fill in a simple form, including name, address, phone number, and area code.	f Ask someone to spell something.	g Spell something aloud.	h State your address, phone number, and area code.	i Write your country of origin.	j Write your first language.

Crossroads 2, Unit 2: Housing

Group Competency Checklist

Teacher________________

Class ________________

NAMES	a Ask about the number and types of rooms.	b Ask about rent and deposits.	c Find out about utilities.	d Identify basic types of housing.	e Identify the total due on monthly bills.	f Ask for information about locations of places in a neighborhood.				

Crossroads 2, Unit 3: Community Services

Group Competency Checklist

Teacher ______________________

Class ______________________

NAMES	a. Fill out an applications for a driver's license or ID.	b. Fill out a money order.	c. Correctly address an envelope including return address.							

Crossroads 2, Unit 4: School

Group Competency Checklist

Teacher ______________________

Class ______________________

NAMES	a State the number of years of previous education and study of English.	b Fill out a form, including birthplace, date of arrival in the U.S., number of years of previous education, and number of years of study of English.	c Give dates, including date of arrival in the U.S.	d Fill out a form, including names, relationships, and ages of family members.			

Crossroads 2, Unit 5: Health

Group Competency Checklist

Teacher____________________

Class ____________________

NAMES	a Identify common injuries.	b Ask about medical treatment.	c Identify common health problems and treatment.	d Read the names of common medicines.	e Read and follow instructions on medicine labels.	f Follow simple instructions for medical treatment.	g Repeat instructions to check your understanding.			

Crossroads 2, Unit 6: Food

Group Competency Checklist

Teacher____________________

Class ____________________

NAMES	a Offer to help someone.	b Respond to offers of help.	c Ask for clarification using basic question words.	d Read prices, weights, measures, for food, and abbreviations.	e State likes and dislikes.					

Crossroads 2, Unit 7: Finding a Job

Group Competency Checklist

Teacher ____________________

Class ____________________

NAMES	a Ask about job openings.	b Set a time for a job interview.	c Answer questions about work experience.	d Fill out a simple job application form.	e Answer questions about work shifts, hours, and starting dates.					

Crossroads 2, Unit 8: On the Job

Group Competency Checklist

Teacher ____________________

Class ____________________

NAMES	a State a need for tools.	b Give simple excuses for lateness or absence.	c Ask to cash a check or money order.	d Show proper ID.	e Apologize for forgetting something.	f Endorse a check or money order.	g Follow spoken instructions about where to put things.			

Crossroads 2, Unit 9: Clothing

Group Competency Checklist

Teacher________________

Class ________________

NAMES	a Name common articles of clothing.	b Ask for the size you need.	c Respond to questions about payment.	d Identify incorrect change and ask for the right amount.	e Give simple descriptions of people.	f Read sizes and prices.				

Crossroads 2, Unit 10: Transportation

Group Competency Checklist

Teacher____________________

Class ____________________

NAMES	a Ask and answer questions about departure and arrival times.	b Read departure and arrival schedules.	c Buy travel tickets, asking about fares.	d Read common traffic and pedestrian signs.	e Give information about the trip from your home country to the U.S.					

Crossroads 2, Unit 1: Introductions

Individual Competency Checklist

See *page x* of *Introduction* for suggestions on using the chart below.

Name ______________________ Date Entered Program ______________________

Class ______________________ Placement Score ______________________

Teacher ______________________

a Introduce yourself.			
b Introduce others.			
c Say where you are from.			
d Say *Goodbye*.			
e Fill in a simple form, including name, address, phone number, and area code.			
f Ask someone to spell something.			
g Spell something aloud.			
h State your address, phone number, and area code.			
i Write your country of origin.			
j Write your first language.			

Crossroads 2, Unit 2: Housing

Individual Competency Checklist

See *page x* of *Introduction* for suggestions on using the chart below.

Name ______________________ Date Entered Program ______________

Class ______________________ Placement Score ______________

Teacher ______________________

a Ask about the number and types of rooms.			
b Ask about rent and deposits.			
c Find out about utilities.			
d Identify basic types of housing.			
e Identify the total due on monthly bills.			
f Ask for information about locations of places in a neighborhood.			

Crossroads 2, Unit 3: Community Services

Individual Competency Checklist

See *page x* of *Introduction* for suggestions on using the chart below.

Name ______________________ Date Entered Program ______________________

Class ______________________ Placement Score ______________________

Teacher ______________________

a Fill out an application for a driver's license or ID.			
b Fill out a money order.			
c Correctly address an envelope including return address.			

Crossroads 2, Unit 4: School

Individual Competency Checklist

See *page x* of *Introduction* for suggestions on using the chart below.

Name ______________________ Date Entered Program ______________________

Class ______________________ Placement Score ______________________

Teacher ______________________

a State the number of years of previous education and study of English.			
b Fill out a form, including birthplace, date of arrival in the U.S., number of years of previous education, and number of years of study of English.			
c Give dates, including date of arrival in the U.S.			
d Fill out a form, including names, relationships, and ages of family members.			

Crossroads 2, Unit 5: Health

Individual Competency Checklist

See *page x* of *Introduction* for suggestions on using the chart below.

Name ____________________ Date Entered Program ____________________

Class ____________________ Placement Score ____________________

Teacher ____________________

a Identify common injuries.			
b Ask about medical treatment.			
c Identify common health problems and treatment.			
d Read the names of common medicines.			
e Read and follow instructions on medicine labels.			
f Follow simple instructions for medical treatment.			
g Repeat instructions to check your understanding.			

Crossroads 2, Unit 6: Food

Individual Competency Checklist

See *page x* of *Introduction* for suggestions on using the chart below.

Name ______________________ Date Entered Program ______________

Class ______________________ Placement Score ______________

Teacher ______________________

a Offer to help someone.			
b Respond to offers of help.			
c Ask for clarification using basic question words.			
d Read prices, weights, measures for food, and abbreviations.			
e State likes and dislikes.			

Crossroads 2, Unit 7: Finding a Job

Individual Competency Checklist

See *page x* of *Introduction* for suggestions on using the chart below.

Name ______________________ Date Entered Program ______________

Class ______________________ Placement Score ______________

Teacher ______________________

a Ask about job openings.			
b Set a time for a job interview.			
c Answer questions about work experience.			
d Fill out a simple job application form.			
e Answer questions about work shifts, hours, and starting dates.			

Crossroads 2, Unit 8: On the Job

Individual Competency Checklist

See *page x* of *Introduction* for suggestions on using the chart below.

Name ______________________ Date Entered Program ______________

Class ______________________ Placement Score ______________

Teacher ______________________

a State a need for tools.			
b Give simple excuses for lateness or absence.			
c Ask to cash a check or money order.			
d Show proper ID.			
e Apologize for forgetting something.			
f Endorse a check or money order.			
g Follow spoken instructions about where to put things.			

Crossroads 2, Unit 9: Clothing

Individual Competency Checklist

See *page x* of *Introduction* for suggestions on using the chart below.

Name ______________________ Date Entered Program ______________________

Class ______________________ Placement Score ______________________

Teacher ______________________

a Name common articles of clothing.			
b Ask for the size you need.			
c Respond to questions about payment.			
d Identify incorrect change and ask for the right amount.			
e Give simple descriptions of people.			
f Read sizes and prices.			

Crossroads 2, Unit 10: Employment

Individual Competency Checklist

See *page x* of *Introduction* for suggestions on using the chart below.

Name ____________________ Date Entered Program ____________________

Class ____________________ Placement Score ____________________

Teacher ____________________

a Ask and answer questions about departure and arrival times.			
b Read departure and arrival schedules.			
c Buy travel tickets, asking about fares.			
d Read common traffic and pedestrian signs.			
e Give information about the trip from your home country to the U.S.			